Lichen Inventory Synthesis

Western Arctic National Parklands and Arctic Network, Alaska

Natural Resource Technical Report NPS/AKR/ARCN/NRTR—2010/385

Emily A Holt

342 East 200 North
Logan, UT 84321

Peter N Neitlich

National Park Service
41A Wandling Road
Winthrop, WA 98862

November 2010

U.S. Department of the Interior
National Park Service
Natural Resource Program Center
Fort Collins, Colorado

The National Park Service, Natural Resource Program Center publishes a range of reports that address natural resource topics of interest and applicability to a broad audience in the National Park Service and others in natural resource management, including scientists, conservation and environmental constituencies, and the public.

The Natural Resource Technical Report Series is used to disseminate results of scientific studies in the physical, biological, and social sciences for both the advancement of science and the achievement of the National Park Service mission. The series provides contributors with a forum for displaying comprehensive data that are often deleted from journals because of page limitations.

All manuscripts in the series receive the appropriate level of peer review to ensure that the information is scientifically credible, technically accurate, appropriately written for the intended audience, and designed and published in a professional manner. This report received formal peer review by subject-matter experts who were not directly involved in the collection, analysis, or reporting of the data, and whose background and expertise put them on par technically and scientifically with the authors of the information.

Views, statements, findings, conclusions, recommendations, and data in this report do not necessarily reflect views and policies of the National Park Service, U.S. Department of the Interior. Mention of trade names or commercial products does not constitute endorsement or recommendation for use by the U.S. Government.

This report is available from the Arctic I&M Network (http://www.nature.nps.gov/im/units/ARCN) and the Natural Resource Publications Management website (http://www.nature.nps.gov/publications/NRPM).

Please cite this publication as:

Holt, E. A. and P. N. Neitlich. 2010. Lichen inventory synthesis: Western Arctic National Parklands and Arctic Network, Alaska. Natural Resource Technical Report NPS/AKR/ARCN/NRTR—2010/385. National Park Service, Fort Collins, Colorado.

NPS 953/105821, November 2010

Contents

                                                                                           Page

Figures...v

Tables vi

Appendixes vii

Abstract viii

Acknowledgments..ix

Introduction 1

Study Area 3

Methods..5

    Sampling Designs 5

    Data Collection 7

    Additional Variables...9

    Diversity 11

    Data Adjustments..11

    Analyses..13

Results..15

    Diversity 15

    Community Structure..15

    Park Differences 18

Discussion 19

    Elevation-Moisture Gradient 19

    Substrate Gradient 19

    BELA v. Other Park Units..21

Conclusions..23

Recommendations... 24

Literature Cited 27

Figures

Page

Figure 1. Map of the study area in northwestern Alaska, including the five ARCN park units (BELA, CAKR, GAAR, KOVA and NOAT)... 1

Figure 2. Species-area curves comparing large, circular 0.38-ha plots to small, rectangular 0.0036-ha plots.. 12

Figure 3. NMS ordination of 235 surveyed plots (249 plot subset minus outliers) in species space. 17

Tables

Page

Table 1. List of projects whose data and collections are contained within this report.................... 2

Table 2. Model and accuracy of GPS used in the field. 7

Table 3. Characteristics of sampled plots in four ARCN park units used in gradient analyses. Mean values in original units and standard errors in parentheses. 9

Table 4. Lichen taxa used for height estimates. 10

Table 5. Noteworthy collections of new or rare taxa to North America (N Am) or Alaska (AK). 16

Table 6. Pairwise comparisons in lichen community composition among parks using MRPP. 18

Appendixes

Page

Appendix 1. Lichen species list from 445 sites within ARCN, including 351 macrolichens, 138 microlichens and 2 basidiolichens. 32

Abstract

We describe lichen community structure and its relation to environment in five national parks within the Arctic Network (ARCN) in northwestern Alaska. We found a total of 117 lichen genera and 491 unique lichen taxa from 264 0.38-ha plots, 107 32-m^2 plots and 74 opportunistic surveys. Jackknife estimates adjusted our macrolichen gamma diversity from 351 to an expected 416 (first-order) or 449 (second-order) macrolichen species. Three primary gradients in lichen species composition were related to elevation and moisture; substrate pH; and park unit. The strongest community gradient was associated with moisture availability and differences between alpine and lowland habitats. Along this ordination axis, lowland, wet sites dominated by graminoids and shrubs graded into drier, steep and rocky alpine sites at high elevations. Shallow bedrock and the sloping nature of alpine sites prevent formation of permafrost within their soils; the resulting windscoured, cold, dry conditions limit vascular plant growth and promote favorable lichen habitat. The second strongest gradient, related to substrate pH, was driven by the presence of *Sphagnum* moss that overwhelmed any bedrock chemical signal at one end and calcareous alpine sites that exposed overlying vegetation to its alkaline chemistry at the opposing end. Moreover, this axis was associated with a trend of decreasing diversity with increasing substrate alkalinity. The final community gradient clearly separated Bering Land Bridge National Preserve (BELA) from all other park units. The paucity of calcareous substrates and minimal woody plants caused lichen communities in BELA to cluster apart from habitats present throughout the remainder of ARCN. Gradients evident in this ARCN-wide analysis mirror those found previously in separate, independent analyses of individual ARCN park units. These similarities underscore that patterns in lichen community composition transcend small geographic scales and apply to large expanses of Arctic Alaska. Information in this study represents a snapshot of macrolichen communities in northwestern Alaska that serves as an important baseline for future comparisons, including long-term monitoring through the Arctic Network.

Acknowledgments

The authors thank Teuvo Ahti, Shanti Berryman, Linda Geiser, Amanda Hardman, Linda Hasselbach, Bruce McCune, Scott Miller, Anaka Mines, Sarah Nunn, Sean Patrick, Roger Rosentreter, Abby Rosso and Alex Rupprecht for their contribution to this project through fieldwork and labwork. Dave Swanson and Sarah Jovan provided helpful reviews that greatly improved this report.

Introduction

The Arctic Network (ARCN) is a network of five national parks in northwestern Alaska (Fig 1.). These parks, including Bering Land Bridge National Preserve (BELA), Cape Krusenstern National Monument (CAKR), Gates of the Arctic National Park and Preserve (GAAR), Kobuk Valley National Park (KOVA) and Noatak National Preserve (NOAT), encompass habitats from the peaks of the Brooks Range westward to the Bering Sea coast. In size, these five parks represent a quarter of all National Park Service lands in the country (~81,500 km^2). ARCN includes some of the most remote, roadless public lands in the US. Its inaccessibility has helped preserve its unique and natural ecosystems; however, its isolation and distance has made the network relatively less studied than more accessible park units elsewhere.

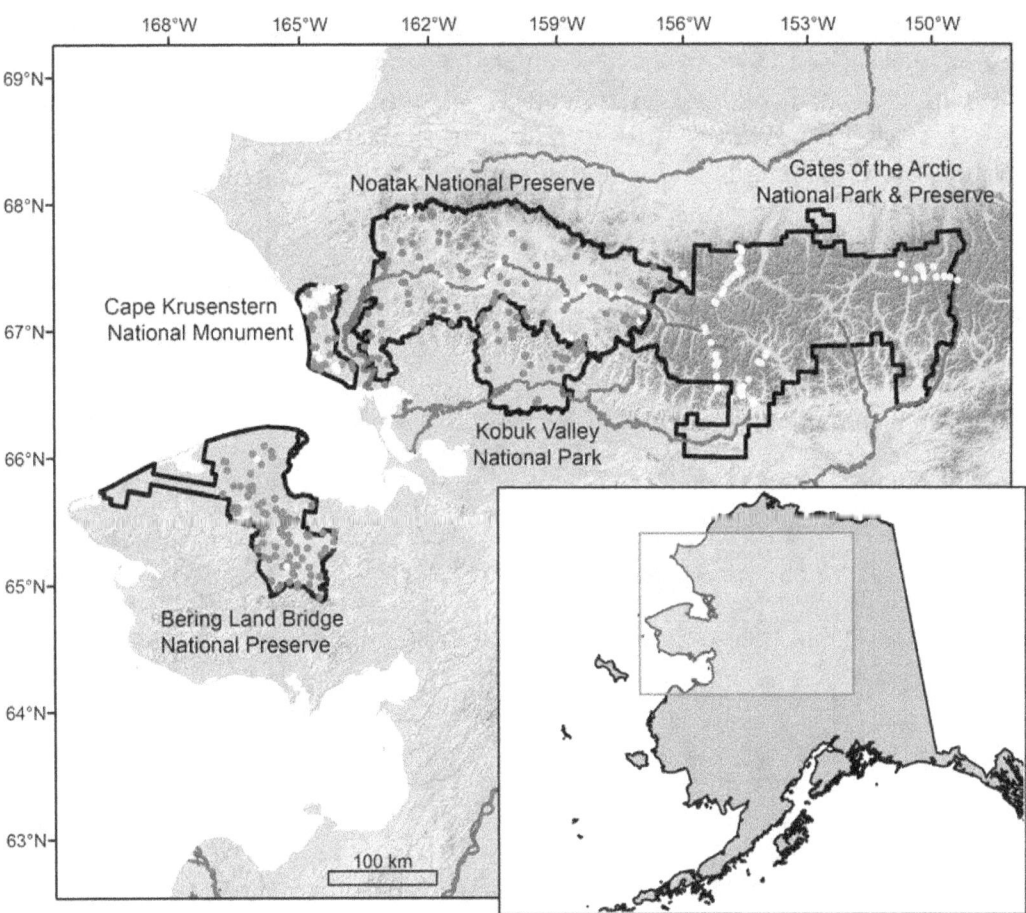

Figure 1. Map of the study area in northwestern Alaska, including the five ARCN park units (BELA, CAKR, GAAR, KOVA and NOAT). Points indicate 445 collection sites sampled between 1996 and 2007. Red circles represent the subset of 249 plots used in the gradient analysis, while yellow circles indicate the remaining 196 plots and surveys reflected in diversity estimates but not in the community analysis.

This report presents a compilation and synthesis of 12 years of lichen sampling in the Arctic Network (Table 1). Lichens contribute a large portion of the biomass and diversity to the Arctic tundra and boreal forested habitats within these parks (Neitlich and Hasselbach 1998; Jorgenson

1

et al. 2004; Holt et al. 2009). Cyanolichens provide a sizable portion of the fixed nitrogen in these nutrient-poor ecosystems (Gunther 1989; Hobara et al. 2006). Arthropods, birds and small mammals use lichens for dwelling or nesting materials (Brodo et al. 2001). Several large mammals, including reindeer, caribou and muskoxen, all rely on lichens for winter and occasional summer forage (Scotter 1964; Ihl and Klein 2001). Despite their remoteness, these lichen communities are increasingly threatened by direct and indirect anthropogenic influences, including climate change, air pollution, grazing by managed reindeer herds, recreation activities and its associated traffic. Several climate projections predict a large loss of tundra ecosystems by 2100 with increasing shrub and forest cover, especially in the Arctic (Walker et al. 2003; Bachelet et al. 2005). These changes would likely represent a negative influence on the terricolous lichen communities pervasive throughout ARCN. Increased knowledge of diversity, distribution and community patterns can provide an additional tool to help managers assess threats to these sensitive communities or protect species at risk. The only large-scale floristic treatment of lichens in northwestern Alaska was part of a larger effort over a quarter of a century ago (Thomson 1984). Since 1996, we have conducted extensive inventories of all macrolichens in these five park units, and collected microlichens (i.e., crustose lichens) opportunistically in parts of NOAT. Goals of the present work were to: 1) document all lichen taxa found on ARCN parklands, and 2) describe ARCN-wide lichen community structure and its relation to environment.

Table 1. List of projects whose data and collections are contained within this report.

Project	Year	Primary Collector(s)	Plot Type[1]	Citation(s)
BELA	2000-2004	Holt, Neitlich	large	Holt et al. 2007, Holt et al. 2008
CAKR06	2006	Berryman, Geiser, Mines, Neitlich	small	Neitlich et al. 2010
CAKR07	2007	Berryman, Rosso	large	Berryman et al. 2010
GAAR	1996-1997	Hasselbach, Neitlich	large, survey	Neitlich and Hasselbach 1998
KOVA	2007	Berryman, Rosso	large	Berryman et al. 2010
NOAT	2004-2005	Ahti, Holt, McCune, Neitlich, Rosentreter	large, survey	Holt et al. 2009, McCune et al. 2009

[1] Plot types: Large = 34.7m-radius circular plots; small = 4x8m plots; survey = opportunistic surveys of non-standard size.

Study Area

The five parks of the Arctic Network are located in northwestern Alaska (65°15'-68°39'N, 149°32'-167°32'W; Fig. 1). The two largest parks, GAAR and NOAT, occupy the central and western Brooks Range. Elevations range from 2,523 m above sea level (asl) on Mt. Igikpak in the Schwatka Mountains to sea level on the Chukchi Sea coast in BELA and CAKR. The Noatak River, the longest National Wild and Scenic River, originates on Mt. Igikpak and traverses westward through both GAAR and NOAT before finally emptying into the Kotzebue Sound of the Chukchi Sea (Milner et al. 2005). The majority of the Noatak watershed lies within ARCN (GAAR, NOAT and CAKR), making it the largest protected watershed in the US (Milner et al. 2005).

The mean annual temperatures in the network range from -5°C to -6°C at low elevations to -10°C to -13°C at high elevations (Daly 2002a, Manley and Daly 2005). Mean July temperatures range from about 15°C at low elevations in the taiga zones of KOVA and GAAR to less than 5°C in the high mountains of GAAR (Manley and Daly 2005). The coastal parks, CAKR and BELA, are buffered by the oceanic influence of the Chukchi Sea, and have average summer temperatures of 7°C (Manley and Daly 2005). Mean January temperatures are approximately -17°C in BELA and CAKR, and around -25°C in inland valleys (Manley and Daly 2005). Climate in ARCN varies with continentality and elevation among parks. In addition, the maritime parks tend to be wetter at low elevations, while the inland parks are drier (Manley and Daly 2005). Mean annual precipitation ranges from about 210mm along the coast to over 900mm at high elevations in the central Brooks Range, with the maximum occurring in late summer (Daly 2002a). The coastal plains of BELA and CAKR generally receive between 200-300mm, while mountains in these parks receive as much as 700mm. In NOAT, the low elevations are drier (<200mm) than the mountains of NOAT and western GAAR (>800mm). Precipation decreases inland, as one travels east from the CAKR coast into the high elevations in GAAR; the high mountains of eastern GAAR receive the same range of precipitation as the low hills of CAKR (Daly 2002b).

ARCN also hosts tremendous variation in geology, including calcareous and noncalcareous rocks of sedimentary, metamorphic and volcanic origins (Moore et al. 1994). The maritime parks (BELA and CAKR) were not glaciated during the Pleistocene, while the more mountainous portions of inland parks (KOVA, NOAT and GAAR) were formerly covered by alpine glaciers (Péwé 1975; Hamilton 2009). Lower portions of these inland parks, occupying the southern slopes of the Brooks Range, mark the northern extent of the boreal forest in Alaska (Viereck et al. 1992; Edwards et al. 2003). Forested communities in ARCN are often dominated by *Picea glauca* (Moench) Voss and *Betula papyrifera* Marsh. Arctic tundra, however, blankets most landscapes within these five parks. Tall shrub communities exist within ARCN, but are far less widespread than low or dwarf shrub communities. Tall shrubs consist of *Salix* spp., *Betula glandulosa* Michx. and *Alnus crispa* (Ait.) Pursh; while subshrubs include *B. nana* L., *Vaccinium* spp., *Arctostaphylos* spp., *Empetrum nigrum* L., *Cassiope tetragona* L., *Dryas octopetala* L. and *Ledum palustre* var. *decumbens* (Ait.) Hultén. The herb layer contains mixed *Eriophorum* spp. and *Carex* spp.. The dominant mosses are *Pleurozium schreberi* (Brid.) Mitt. and *Hylocomium splendens* (Hedw.) Schimp., with various *Sphagnum* spp. The lichen flora is dominated by species from the genera *Cladina*, *Cladonia*, *Cetraria*, *Peltigera* and *Stereocaulon*.

Methods

Sampling Designs

Lichen sampling across ARCN primarily used a stratified random sampling design. Stratifying variables included geographic information systems (GIS) land cover data (e.g., BELA, CAKR06, CAKR07, KOVA, and NOAT), geology (e.g., CAKR07, KOVA) and geographic delineators (e.g., BELA, NOAT, CAKR06). All studies, except GAAR, used a one- or two-way stratification; in GAAR, all plots were opportunistic and subjectively placed.

Each park had, until recently, an independent land classification (Markon and Wesser 1997, 1998; Jorgensen et al. 2004) that was used in the stratification process. Although individual land classifications share many similarities to those from other parks and are based on similar data, each is independent. Future network-wide efforts will need to rely on spatial modeling or create new network-wide strata if post-stratification approaches are desired. We chose land cover variables as the primary stratification principle in all studies to focus the sampling effort in lichen-rich areas or to minimize the noise in community differences of uncommon or lichen-poor areas. All vegetated strata in each land classification were sampled in all studies except BELA and CAKR06. In BELA, pilot studies demonstrated that only four land cover types (*Dwarf Shrub-Lichen Dominated*, *Mesic-Dry Herbaceous*, *Open Low Shrub-Dwarf Birch/Ericaceous* and *Sparse Vegetation*) had a minimum average lichen cover of 10%, thus sampling was restricted to these cover types. In CAKR06, only the two dominant community types (*Upland Moist Dwarf Birch-Ericaceous Shrub* and *Upland Moist Dwarf Birch-Tussock Shrub*) along the Red Dog Haul Road were sampled. To minimize the total number of sampling possibilities within each land cover classification, classes were aggregated within NOAT (McCune et al. 2009), CAKR and KOVA. Notably, although classes were reclassified, all 15 strata in the original NOAT land classification were sampled and likewise with the 23 strata in CAKR and 16 strata in KOVA.

Three of the projects implemented a two-way random stratification specifically using geographic delineators and land cover data. In the CAKR06 study, seven buffer lines (at 10, 50, 100, 300, 1000, 2000 and 4000m from the edge of the road) were created in GIS parallel to the Red Dog Mine haul road (Delong Mountain Transportation System or DMTS). Along the 10m buffer line on the north side of the DMTS, three points were randomly located within each the two targeted land cover classes. Six points were chosen in the same manner along the 10m buffer line on the south side of the road. This procedure was then followed on the remaining buffer lines (six lines north and six lines south of the DMTS). Of the random points generated on the buffer lines greater than 10m from the road, only those most proximal to the first random point on the 10m buffer were selected for sampling. The goal was to align points (which overlayed the seven buffer distances and two land cover classes) into an approximate 4000m-"transect" perpendicular to the road. The design was balanced by an equal number of plots in each of the two targeted cover classes on each side of the road.

Similarly, we created geographic blocks in BELA and NOAT to balance the sampling effort across the area of interest. In BELA, the far northern portion of the preserve was wetlands depauperate in lichens, thus purposefully excluded in our sampling. The central portion of BELA was divided into approximately twenty-one roughly equal-area (~ 400 km^2) geographic blocks in GIS. Within each geographic block, four points from each cover type were randomly selected. This sampling scheme, however, was only used in the 2002-2004 effort; the twenty BELA plots completed in 2000-2001 used a one-way stratification of land cover data only. In NOAT, the preserve was divided into four geographic blocks demarcated by preserve boundaries and physiographic regions created by the Noatak and Nimiuktuk Rivers. Within each geographic block, several points from each of the seven aggregated cover type were randomly located. In 2004, sampling emphasis was focused on visiting every cover type within the two western geographic blocks (to maximize limited time and money). Based on these data, we then used adaptive sampling to determine the sampling intensity within each of the seven cover types for our effort in 2005. The number of plots in each geographic block was roughly equal, while each cover type was represented proportionate to its average species richness based on 2004 estimates (McCune et al. 2009).

Sampling designs of the remaining two projects, KOVA and CAKR07, were focused on capturing variability in vegetation and geology. The land cover classification inclusive of CAKR and BELA (Jorgenson et al. 2004) categorized the landscape according to vegetation as well as alkalinity in areas where exposed bedrock or parent material influences overlying vegetation. In CAKR07, we aggregated the 23 vegetated land cover classes present in CAKR into 14 new strata. Three points were randomly selected in each of these new strata. Conversely, the KOVA land cover classification (Markon and Wesser 1998) reflected only vegetation. To incorporate geologic factors, the KOVA study implemented a two-way stratification of geology (i.e., Ecoregion Subsection Lithology from Swanson and Spencer 2001) and land cover data. The original 16 vegetated land cover classes were reclassified into eight new classes. Geology delineations were also aggregated into two possible subtypes: calcareous and acidic. Where applicable, three points were randomly located within each unique geology-land cover combination.

Barring three exceptions, all plots were randomly located using the AlaskaPak (National Park Service 2010) extension's random point generator in ArcGIS. This tool randomly selects a point within the strata of interest. Each point was screened to consider only those that were buffered by a block of at least eight same-stratum pixels (i.e., a minimum cluster of nine contiguous 30m-pixels) to avoid isolated pixels that are frequently misclassified. Large-scale misclassifications, however, can be overlooked in this screening and were occasionally discovered upon arriving at the site. In these cases, misclassified plots were discarded, unsampled and substituted with alternate random points. The first exception to the random location of plots was in KOVA and CAKR07, when all potential points of some strata were mapped incorrectly. To obtain sufficient representation in each vegetation stratum, judgment plots—sites we actively sought to corresponded to the typical habitat for this stratum—were located (2 in CAKR and 16 in KOVA) non-randomly. Secondly, GAAR study points were selected arbitrarily rather than randomly, due to accessibility constraints. The final exception to data collected non-randomly was the opportunistic surveys conducted in parts of NOAT and GAAR. These sampling efforts were done in areas of geological or lichenological interest or due to their proximity to the Noatak River.

Data Collection

Lichen community composition was evaluated using a variant of a long-term lichen monitoring protocol (USDA/Forest Service FIA Program's Lichen Indicator) implemented in previous studies (McCune et al. 1997; McCune 2000). Designed for temperate forests and applied to thousands of plots in the US, these protocols focus on epiphytic macrolichens. Although the few forested sites we visited could implement these protocols, most sites lacked trees. In tundra environments, we sampled terricolous and saxicolous macrolichens and epiphytic macrolichens on shrubs. Preservation of key elements of the technique facilitated region-wide comparisons included in the present study.

In all studies except CAKR06, most sample units were circular fixed-area plots with a 34.7-meter radius (0.38 ha). We surveyed 98 plots in BELA, 29 in CAKR, 11 in GAAR, 38 in KOVA and 88 in NOAT. Trained lichenologists searched all substrates for a maximum of two hours, recording all species and collecting vouchers of any unknown specimens. Each species encountered was assigned an abundance value: 1 = rare (<3 thalli), 2 = uncommon (4-10 thalli), 3 = common (<1% cover but >10 thalli), 4 = abundant (1-5% cover), 5 = prolific (6-25% cover) and 6 = dominant (>26% cover). Vouchers were deposited at Oregon State University Herbarium (OSC), University of Colorado at Boulder (COLO), University of Alaska at Fairbanks Herbarium (ALA) and the NPS Herbaria in Anchorage, Alaska and Winthrop, WA. Lichen determinations were primarily based on Thomson (1984), Goward and others (1994) and Goward (1999).

We attempted to locate plot center precisely at the "target" coordinate for that site. Accessibility limitations (e.g., dangerously steep slope, inadequate landing spot for helicopter, helicopter sitting exactly over the coordinate) hindered some of these efforts. In such cases, plot centers were off-set by walking towards the original plot (or along a random azimuth if walking towards the plot was not possible) following a random distance. Plot center was then recorded after the GPS unit (see Table 2) acquired an adequate satellite coverage with the lowest possible horizontal error. Plot edges were marked with flagging or pin flags. Photographs were taken of most plots, excluding the GAAR plots which have no accompanying pictures. Photos were usually taken from plot center (azimuth varies) to capture the "typical" landcape at that plot and any other interesting landmarks. The Lichen Inventory Photo Archive contains 811 photos (369 from BELA, 219 from CAKR, 53 from KOVA and 170 from NOAT).

Table 2. Model and accuracy of GPS used in the field.

Project	GPS Receiver Type	Horizontal Accuracy (m)
BELA	Garmin 12Map	< 15
CAKR06	Trimble GeoXT	0.4 – 1.1
CAKR07	Trimble Geo XH 2005	0.1 – 0.7
GAAR	Garmin GPS 48	< 15
KOVA	Trimble Geo XH 2005	0.1 – 0.7
NOAT[1]	Garmin 12Map	< 15
	Garmin Map 76S	< 3

[1]Garmin 12Map used in 2004 and Garmin Map 76S used in 2005.

Environmental measurements included topographic variables as well as percent cover of various aspects of the vegetation (see Table 3). Slope was determined with a clinometer and averaged for upslope and downslope. Using a compass with the appropriate declination for that year, aspect was estimated. Aspect and slope were transformed into estimates of potential annual direct incident radiation, based on the maximum northern latitude the computations can handle (60°N; McCune and Keon 2002, Equation 3). We also measured the abundance of other vegetative and site characteristics using ocular estimates of cover (<1 – 100%; Table 3). Site characteristics estimated included: bare duff (obvious litter present on the soil surface); bare mineral soil (soil that was not covered in plant litter and not inclusive of rocks); exposed rock (including large boulders to exposed bedrock to small pebbles that covered large portions of the plot) and water cover (standing water not attributed to fleeting weather events). The vegetation layers we estimated included: bryophytes (both liverworts and mosses); forbs (herbaceous, non-graminoid plants, including *Dryas*); graminoids (grasses, sedges and rushes); subshrubs (woody plants < 1m); tall shrubs (woody plants > 1m, primarily alder and willow) and trees (mostly spruce).

In addition to the above described lichen surveys, 107 smaller plots were sampled in CAKR (CAKR06) to focus efforts on heavy metal pollution along the DMTS. Rectangular plots (4 x 8m) were established using the two-way stratification of distance from the road and land cover data, specified above. Lichen abundance was assessed with a point-intercept method using 100 points spaced on a rectangular grid. Within each 4 x 8m plot, 10 parallel lines were spaced 80cm apart on the long side of the plot, along which there were 10 points spaced every 40cm. Species not encountered on a point-count but observed in trace abundances within the plot were recorded and assigned an abundance value of 0.1. Futhermore, 74 opportunistic surveys were conducted in parts of NOAT (22 surveys) and GAAR (52 surveys). These surveys were not confined within plots; rather general collection of an undefined area sought to maximize species capture in unique habitats that fell beyond the stratified sample. Electronic copies of the raw community and environmental data are available on NPS Data Store, and a hardcopy of the data as well as field notes and any other significant project documentation will be archived with NPS collections at the Alaska Regional Office in Anchorage. Tissue of the moss *Hylocomium splendens* was also collected for elemental analysis from all 38 KOVA, 136 CAKR and 61 NOAT plots; results of this study are reported elsewhere (Neitlich, unpublished data).

Table 3. Characteristics of sampled plots in four ARCN park units used in gradient analyses. Mean values in original units and standard errors in parentheses. Different letters indicate statistically different cover types (α = 0.05) using transformed variables in ANOVA. "All" represents the ARCN-wide average across all four park units, weighted by area of the unit (weighted SE in parentheses).

	BELA	CAKR	KOVA	NOAT	ALL
SAMPLE SIZES					
No. plots	94	29	38	88	249[1]
Area (~km[2])	11,270	2,670	7,090	26,560	47590
LICHEN COMMUNITIES					
Mean alpha diversity[2]	22.5 (0.94)[a]	29.3 (2.75)[b]	37.8 (2.80)[c]	25.9 (1.19)[a,b]	26.9 (0.83)
Gamma diversity[2]	149	171	225	203	302
Beta diversity[2]	5.6	4.8	5.0	6.8	10.2
Lichen cover (%)	28.3 (2.16)[a]	4.07 (1.17)[b]	14.8 (3.25)[c]	6.84 (0.96)[b,c]	16.2 (4.26)
SUCCESSIONAL MEASURES					
Lichen height (cm)	7.29 (0.14)[a]	3.72 (0.07)[b]	4.83 (0.11)[b]	5.32 (0.40)[b]	5.42 (0.65)
Successional score[3]	2.18 (0.01)[a]	2.01 (0.01)[b]	1.99 (0.01)[b]	2.04 (0.01)[b]	2.04 (0.03)
SITE CHARACTERISTICS					
Bare duff (%)	2.44 (0.27)[a]	6.75 (2.10)[a,b]	14.0 (3.32)[b,c]	18.20 (1.88)[c]	11.5 (3.24)
Bare mineral soil (%)	3.70 (0.83)[a,b]	0.74 (0.26)[a]	2.13 (1.63)[a]	4.45 (0.70)[b]	2.77 (0.63)
Bryophyte cover (%)	14.0 (1.47)[a]	35.3 (6.31)[b]	24.0 (4.53)[a,b]	33.9 (2.94)[b]	23.7 (3.95)
Elevation (m)	244.0 (16.1)[a]	156.0 (25.7)[a]	459.5 (50.0)[b]	461.7 (29.5)[b]	501.4 (77.90)
Exposed rock (%)	13.9 (2.68)[a]	19.5 (5.94)[a,b]	29.3 (5.96)[b]	18.3 (3.47)[a,b]	23.5 (3.75)
Incident Radiation[4]	-0.69 (0.01)	-0.60 (0.04)	-0.63 (0.05)	-0.68 (0.03)	-0.65 (0.02)
Slope (deg)	3.77 (0.50)[a]	9.15 (2.01)[b,c]	14.3 (1.91)[c]	8.55 (1.05)[b]	10.6 (2.47)
Water cover (%)	2.18 (0.40)[u]	1.80 (1.27)[a,u]	0.01 (0.01)[u]	0.64 (0.20)[u]	0.72 (0.54)
VASCULAR COMMUNITIES					
Forb cover (%)	10.76 (1.35)[a]	4.93 (2.58)[b]	3.37 (1.00)[b]	14.8 (1.99)[a]	6.91 (2.51)
Graminoid cover (%)	32.50 (2.48)[b]	23.6 (5.02)[b]	9.87 (2.69)[a]	31.6 (2.99)[b]	19.2 (6.27)
Subshrub cover (%)	21.1 (1.66)[a]	35.5 (4.47)[b]	37.3 (4.59)[b]	35.6 (2.05)[b]	33.1 (3.56)
Tall shrub cover (%)	9.00 (1.11)	11.5 (4.06)	8.71 (2.57)	13.2 (2.15)	9.61 (0.73)
Tree cover (%)	0.00 (0.00)[a]	1.54 (1.07)[a,b]	5.56 (2.00)[b]	3.30 (1.16)[b]	3.68 (1.32)

[1]Diversity estimates reflect all 249 plots, while all other variables reflect only 235, excluding the outliers.
[2]Alpha diversity is species richness per plot, gamma diversity is richness for the whole sampling effort, and beta diversity is a measure of composition change among plots.
[3]Successional scores range between one and three.
[4]Calculation based on slope, aspect and latitude, and units are MJ/cm[2]/yr.

Additional Variables

We estimated the successional status of all plots in BELA, CAKR, KOVA and NOAT using two independent methods: lichen height and successional scores based on lichen community composition. Lichen height has been used elsewhere to measure the response of lichens to disturbance (e.g., Ahti 1959; Steen 1965). This measure assumes that grazing and other ground disturbances can result in shorter lichens compared to tall lichens that inhabit undisturbed sites. Due to variation in frequency and abundance of lichen taxa among parks, all the same species could not be consistently used for height estimates. We measured the length of nine species or isomorphs where available (Table 4). In the field, we walked a random number of steps from plot center and searched for individuals of the species of interest. Occasionally taxa used for height measurements were rare on a plot; thus, the search was not random or in some cases measurements were not possible. Lichens were carefully pulled from the lichen mat, or the mat was excavated to ensure the majority of the thallus was extracted (although we acknowledge there is inevitably some lichen broken off and unmeasured at the base). Lichens were laid on a ruler and measured to the nearest millimeter. Our goal was to sample five heights per species per plot. We combined these measurements into a single variable of average lichen height for each plot. Height estimates were made for each park, independent of all other parks.

Table 4. Lichen taxa used for height estimates. Pluses indicate unadjusted species used in height estimates, and "A" indicates species measured whose heights were adjusted.

Species	BELA	CAKR07	KOVA	NOAT
Alectoria ochroleuca	+	+		
Alectoria nigricans	A	+		
Bryocaulon divergens	A			
Cladina arbuscula	+			
Cladina arbuscula/ mitis[1]		A	+	+
Cladina rangiferina				+
Cladina stygia	+	A	A	
Cetraria cucullata	+	+	A	+
Cetraria islandica			+	
Cetraria laevigata	+		+	
Cetraria laevigata/ islandica[1]		+		+
Thamnolia subuliformis / vermicularis[1]		+	A	

[1]Isomorphs lumped in the field.

In all parks except NOAT, we could not use simple averages because growth rates differed among species. To assess species' growth rates, on a park-by-park basis, we pooled the height data from all species into a variable of pooled height for each plot. Then individual species' heights were regressed against the pooled height of all target species available for each plot. Slopes greater than one indicate that a particular species grows faster than average, while slopes less than one indicate slower than average growth rates. Seventeen species in the four parks had a slope near one and did not require adjustment (Table 4). Alternatively, several species had slopes fairly different than one and consequently were adjusted (Table 4). Regression coefficients [target species height = (growth rate or slope) x (pooled height) + intercept] were used to calculate adjusted heights for the seven species whose growth rates were slower than the other species in the park, such that each species would have similar growth rates. To calculate average adjusted lichen height in a particular plot, the intercept from the regression was subtracted from the observed height value for that plot, and then divided by the slope. The final value for lichen height for a given plot was the average height of all species available at each site, including the unadjusted species and adjusted species together.

Finally, we created a variable to represent the successional status of each plot. In a previous study, we categorized 46 species into early, mid- or late successional stages using a synthesis of literature reports on succession following grazing and fire (Holt et al. 2006). Each species was assigned a successional species weight of one, two or three to represent these early to late-successional stages, respectively. We used weighted averaging to combine our abundance estimates with these species scores yielding successional plot scores for each site. The possible range of successional scores was from 1.0 to 3.0, to indicate the successional status of the lichen species present on that site.

Diversity

We estimated alpha and gamma diversity for the entire sampling effort of all five park units following McCune and Grace (2002). Alpha diversity was measured as the number of unique lichen taxa per plot, while gamma diversity was the total number of observed species for the entire sampling effort. Furthermore, beta diversity, in addition to alpha and gamma diversity, was estimated in various subsets of the dataset. Beta diversity is the average compositional difference among plots (McCune and Grace 2002). It is calculated as the total number of species from all plots combined divided by the average species richness and all subtracted by one (β_w; Whittaker 1972).

Although our estimates of gamma diversity aimed to approximate the total number of species found throughout ARCN, these measures invariably underestimate the true value (Palmer 1990, 1995). Therefore, we used nonparametric resampling (jackknife) methods in PC-ORD 5 (McCune and Mefford 2005) to more closely approximate the true gamma diversity in ARCN. We used both first-order (Heltshe and Forrester 1983) and second-order (Burnham and Overton 1979, Palmer 1991) jackknife procedures.

Our gamma diversity estimate for the entire sampling effort of 445 plots and surveys across all five park units included both macrolichens and microlichens. Microlichens, however, were only collected purposefully from opportunistic surveys and 20 plots within NOAT. All microlichen collections (see Appendix 1) were excluded from the subset of data used to form jackknife estimates. We hoped this deletion would more accurately portray the "true" number of macrolichens in ARCN, which were comprehensively collected at all sites.

Data Adjustments

Of the 445 sites that were sampled, we chose to use only a subset of 249 plots for the gradient analysis. We excluded four plots in BELA, all 63 sites in GAAR (11 plots and 52 plotless surveys), 107 plots sampled in 2006 from CAKR (CAKR06), and the 22 opportunistic surveys in NOAT. We based the gradient analysis on these 249 plots because of their consistent size (Fig. 2), comprehensive habitat data, and broad range of vegetation types including in the sampling design.

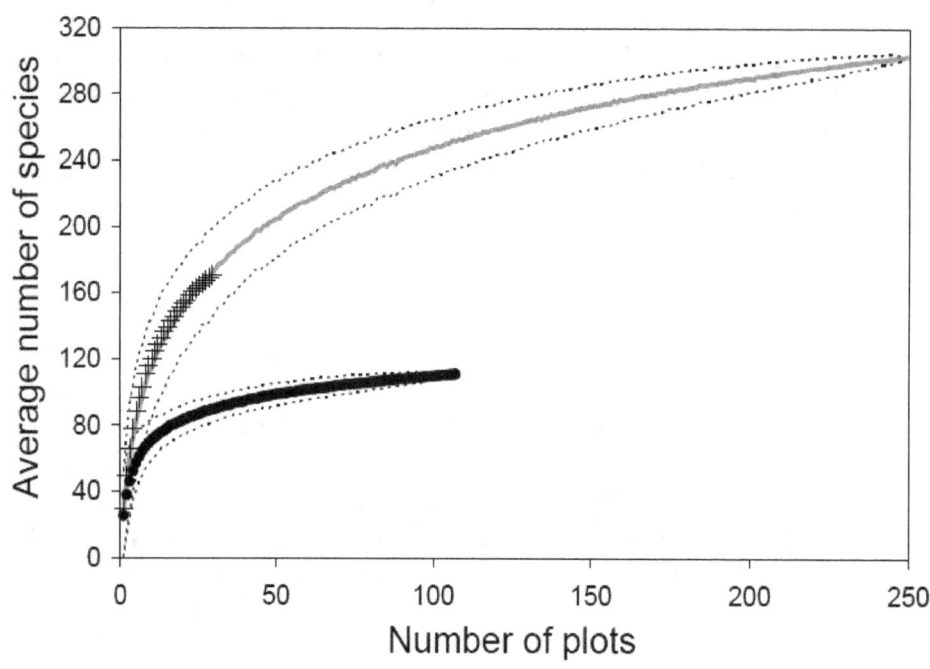

Figure 2. Species-area curves comparing large, circular 0.38-ha plots to small, rectangular 0.0036-ha plots. Solid line indicates curve derived from 249 plots from BELA, CAKR07, KOVA and NOAT combined (all large, circular plots), black circles represent the curve from 107 smaller, rectangular plots from CAKR06, and the pluses indicate the 29 large plots only from CAKR07. Dashed lines represent ±2 standard deviation of the former two curves. Discrepancies between species curves of different sized sampling units (solid line and pluses versus circles), regardless of park, discouraged analysis of all 445 sites together; thus, our gradient analysis includes only plots of similar size and sampling intensity.

We first determined if any plots were multivariate outliers by comparing average community distances between plots. Fourteen of the 249 plots (three from BELA, three from CAKR07, one from KOVA and seven from NOAT) had average Sørensen or Relative Sørensen distances of greater than two standard deviations from the grand mean of all distances. Eleven of these plots were outliers because their sample unit totals and richness values were far lower than average. They had six or fewer unique species and the summed abundance values for all lichen species within the plots was six or less, as compared to 26.9 unique species and an average sample unit total of 59.0 (the average of the summed abundance values for all plots). All eleven of these outliers were found in land cover strata identified as sparsely vegetated, riparian willow habitats or grasslands. In each of these habitats, lichen growth was likely either inhibited by competition by vascular plants, shade or lack of habitat. The remaining three outliers also had lower than average sample unit totals and species richness values, yet only minimally so. Their skewness and kurtosis, however, was much larger than average, due to several very large abundance values (McCune and Grace 2002). In ordinations, the extreme peripheral position of all fourteen plots outside the main point cloud indicated axes gave undue weight to these plots. All fourteen plots were, therefore, removed from all analyses.

Modifications to the community matrix were minimal. The coarse, approximately logarithmic, cover class scale alleviated the need for transformation. However, species documented in less than 5% of plots (185 species total), were deleted from the community matrix to reduce noise and strengthen community relationships (McCune and Grace 2002). Transformations were needed within the environmental matrix, comprised primarily of raw cover values. These cover variables were converted to proportions and arcsine square root transformed for all analyses. This transformation improves normality and reduces skewness within variables measured as proportions (Sokal and Rohlf 1995).

Analyses

The goal of this study was to understand community structure and its relationships to environmental gradients. We used multivariate analysis in PC-ORD 5 (McCune and Mefford 2005). Nonmetric multidimensional scaling (NMS) summarized the multivariate relationships among plots using their species composition (Kruskal 1964; Mather 1976). NMS avoids assumptions of linearity among community variables (McCune and Grace 2002). In addition, NMS allows use of the Sørensen distance measure that is effective with community abundance data. The "slow and thorough" autopilot mode of PC-ORD sought the best fit (lowest stress and instability from multiple random starting configurations), using a maximum of 500 iterations in 250 runs of real data. Statistical significance of the best fit was tested as the proportion of 250 randomized runs with stress less than or equal to the observed stress. Randomizations shuffled elements of the community matrix within species. Ordinations were rigidly rotated to load the strongest environmental variable onto a single axis. The final configuration of sample units in species space consists of ordination scores for each plot on each axis. The coefficient of determination is the proportion of variance in Sørensen distance from the original matrix that was represented by Euclidean distance in the ordination. Linear relationships between ordination scores and environmental variables were depicted as joint plots.

We also wanted to understand differences in lichen community structure among parks. To this end, we measured park distinctness using multi-response permutation procedure (MRPP; Mielke 1984). MRPP is a non-parametric technique which compares within-group homogeneity of *a priori* groupings (i.e., parks) to random expectation. Compositional dissimilarity, measured as Sørensen distance, was averaged within each park unit then pooled across all parks. Statistical significance of these groupings is evaluated by asymptotic approximation (p-value), and the strength or distinctness of each park was evaluated by an A-statistic, the chance-corrected within-group homogeneity. $A = 1$ indicates perfectly homogenous groups, while $A = 0$ indicates within-group heterogeneity equal to chance expectation (McCune and Grace 2002).

Results

Diversity

We documented 117 lichen genera and 491 unique lichen taxa from 445 plots or surveys within the Arctic Network in northwestern Alaska, US (Appendix 1). 351 of these taxa were macrolichens, representing our macrolichen gamma diversity estimate for all five park units combined. Jackknife estimates adjusted this value to an expected 416 (first-order) or 449 (second-order) macrolichen species potentially occurring throughout ARCN. The most frequently occurring lichens included *Cetraria cucullata*, *Cladonia amaurocraea*, *Cetraria laevigata*, *Cetraria islandica* and *Cladina stygia*. These same five taxa and *Cetraria nivalis* had the greatest average abundance. The average species richness was 25.0 per sample unit. This value, however, reflects two different sized sampling unit (large, circular or small, rectangular plots) and differing sampling intensities. Consequently, the subset of 249 (0.38-ha circular) plots from BELA, CAKR, KOVA and NOAT averaged 26.9 species per plot. Following deletion of outliers and species occurring in less than 5% of subset plots, the average species richness was 25.4. The beta diversity for the four-park data subset, 10.2, was quite heterogeneous. This compositional change among plots was greatly reduced ($\beta_w = 3.6$) after deleting outlier plots and rare taxa.

Of the 491 unique species from the entire sampling effort, 351 were macrolichens, 138 were microlichens and 2 were basidiolichens (Appendix 1). Rarity classes based on plot sampling, as outlined in McCune and others (2009) are: abundant (> 50% of plots); common (10-50%); occasional (3-9%) and uncommon (< 3% of plots). Five of the 491 species were considered abundant, 71 were common, 65 were occasional and 350 were uncommon (Appendix 1). Eight taxa were unique to BELA (i.e., occurred only in BELA and no other park units), 12 were unique to CAKR, 24 were unique to GAAR, 23 were unique to KOVA and 173 were unique to NOAT (73% of these 173 species were crusts, attributed mainly to the opportunistic surveys in NOAT). Eighty-four lichen species were observed in all five park units.

To further investigate the rarity of the 350 uncommon taxa, we also queried the status and distribution of each species within resources currently published online (NPLichen; PLANTS Database; Esslinger's North American Lichen Checklist; Panarctic Lichen Checklist) or in print (Thomson 1984; Goward et al. 1994; Goward 1999; Brodo et al. 2001). Noteworthy collections from this study include sixteen lichen taxa new to North America, new to Alaska or rare in North America or Alaska (Table 5).

Community Structure

The three-axis solution recommended by NMS was stronger than expected by chance, based on a randomization test ($p = 0.004$). The best solution yielded a final stress value of 16.9. The final instability was 0.01 and there were 500 iterations in the final solution. Cumulatively, these three axes represented 83.9% of the community variation (Fig. 3).

Table 5. Noteworthy collections of new or rare taxa to North America (N Am) or Alaska (AK). Dashes represent sources[1] who do not report the presence or distribution of a certain species. "Y" indicates the species' presence in a particular source, and where available further details of the species' distribution are provided.

	NPLichen	PLANTS	Esslinger	Thomson	NAmerica	Panarctic	comments/citations
New to North America							
Cladonia ilibifera	–	–	–	–	–	Taimyr Peninsula	Recently documented as new to N Am (McCune et al. 2009)
Cladonia nitens	–	–	Y	–	–	–	Recently documented as new to N Am (McCune et al. 2009)
Hypogymnia castanea	–	–	–	–	–	–	New sp restricted to Seward Pen (McCune 2008)
New to Alaska							
Anzina carneonivea	–	Y	Y	–	–	–	Only other N Am collection from S BC (Goward et al. 1996)
Cladonia ecmocyna ssp. occidentalis	–	Y	Y	–	S Canada	–	Goward (1999) reports N to BC, but no mention of AK
Leucocarpia biatorella	–	–	Y	–	–	–	Recently documented as new to arctic Am (McCune et al. 2009)
Melanelia agnata	–	Y	Y	–	–	Ellesmere; Severnaya Zemlya	Known from Canada/ and MT (Westberg et al. 2004); Goward et al. (1994) reports is incompletely circumboreal, S to BC
Ramalina sinensis	continental	Y	Y	–	Canada	–	Other reports spread throughout cont US, but not this far N
Rhizocarpon rubescens	continental	–	Y	–	Great Lakes; E coast	–	Other reports all eastern and further south
Rare to Alaska or North America							
Cladonia uliginosa	AK	–	Y	–	–	Alaska North	One previous record from N Am include AK Peninsula (Ahti 1998)
Collema curtisporum	continental	Y	Y	–	–	–	One previous record in S AK (Hutchinson and McCune 2001) and not reported in Goward et al. (1994)
Multiclavula vernalis	continental	Y	Y	–	only E US	–	Other reports all from eastern US
Rhizocarpon cumulatum	–	Y	Y	Y	–	–	First locality beyond type (McCune et al. 2009)
Stereocaulon alpestre	–	–	–	–	–	Chukotka S/E; Central Canadian Arctic	Lamb (1977) calls "common and widely distributed", but apparently little documented/recognized
Stereocaulon wrightii	–	–	not in N Am	Y	–	–	Apparently little documented/recognized
Xanthomendoza borealis	–	–	Y	–	rare arctic	Greenland	One previous record from SW AK (Lindblom and Søchting 2008)

[1]Data sources: NPLichen 2009, USDA 2009 , Esslinger 2008, Thomson 1984, 1998, Brodo et al. 2001, Panarctic Lichen Checklist 2006

16

The first axis represented 25.9% of the lichen community variation. The environmental variables with the strongest positive linear correlations with this axis were latitude (large axis one value corresponded to more northern latitudes; $r = 0.63$), duff cover ($r = 0.50$), tree cover ($r = 0.48$), longitude (large axis one value corresponded to more eastern longitudes; $r = 0.44$) and bryophyte cover ($r = 0.44$). Ordered by decreasing strength of the relationship, *Cetraria pinastri*, *Nephroma bellum*, *Peltigera leucophlebia* and *Cladonia chlorophaea* were positively associated with axis one. Negative associations with this axis included both successional measures (successional scores, $r = -0.63$ and lichen height, $r = -0.25$) and overall lichen cover ($r = -0.62$). Some of the strongest lichens negatively related to this axis were *Cetraria cucullata*, *Sphaerophorus globosus*, *C. laevigata*, *Alectoria nigricans* and *Bryocaulon divergens*.

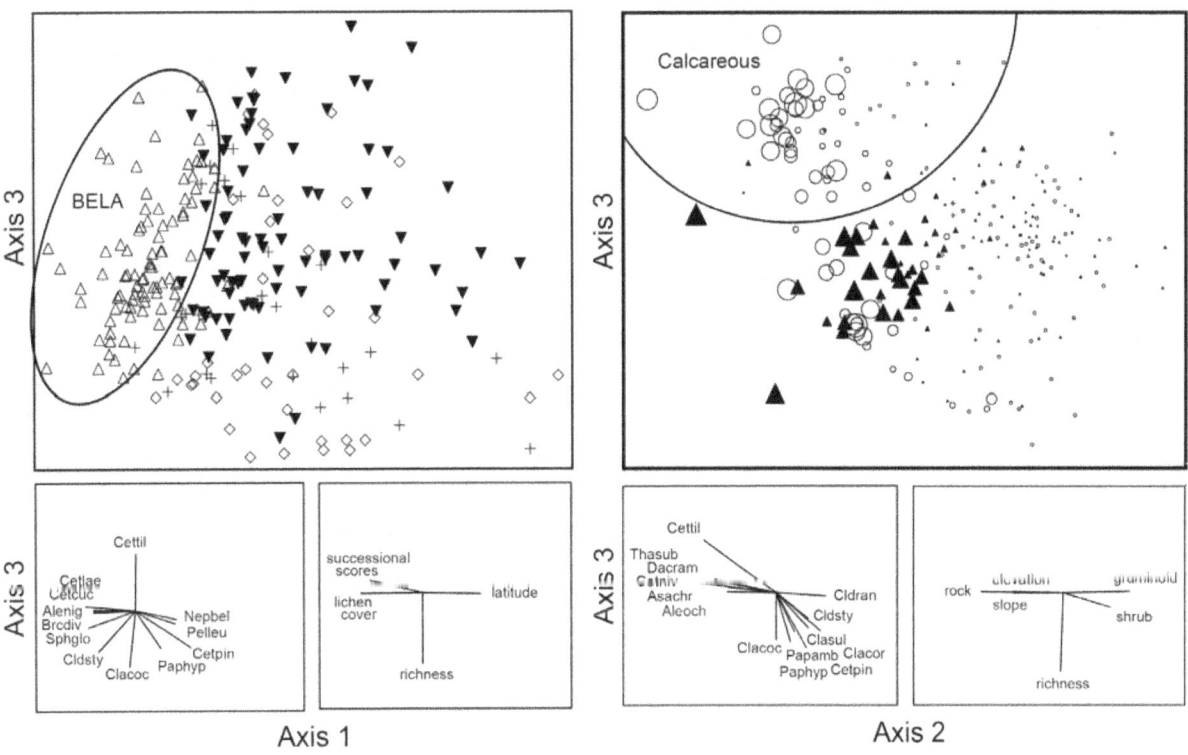

Figure 3. NMS ordination of 235 surveyed plots (249 plot subset minus outliers) in species space. Axis one and three were rigidly rotated -10° and lines represent joint plots of species and environmental variables (r^2 cutoff = 0.25, vector scaling = 125%). The three panels to the left depict axis one and three, while the three panels to the right depict axis two and three. Lichen species codes are listed in Appendix 1. Relevant environmental variables include: lichen successional scores, total lichen cover, lichen species richness, latitude, rock cover, elevation, slope, shrub cover and graminoid cover. Plots in the upper left diagram are coded by park unit, where: Δ: BELA; +: CAKR; ◊: KOVA; ▼: NOAT. The ellipse roughly encloses the cluster of BELA plots along axis 1. Plots in the upper right diagram are coded by substrate (O: calcareous; ▲: non-calcareous bedrock) and their symbol size is scaled relative to rock cover (i.e., smallest symbols indicate zero rock cover, while larger symbols have greater rock cover). The ellipse roughly encloses the cluster of plots underlain by calcareous bedrock with high rock cover.

Axis two represented almost half the variation, 39.6%. Strong positive environmental correlations included graminoid ($r = 0.64$), shrub ($r = 0.54$) and bryophyte cover ($r = 0.48$). Lichen species most positively related to axis two were *Cladina rangiferina*, *Cladonia cornuta*,

17

C. sulfurina and *Cladina stygia*. Lichens strongly associated with the opposing negative portion of this gradient included *Cetraria nivalis*, *C. tilesii*, *Thamnolia subuliformis*, *Dactylina ramulosa*, *Alectoria ochroleuca* and *Asahinea chrysantha*. Rock cover ($r = -0.71$), elevation ($r = -0.55$), slope ($r = -0.55$) and bare soil cover ($r = -0.45$) were also negatively correlated with axis two.

Axis three represented the least community variation, 18.4%, in this solution. Most environmental variables were weakly correlated with axis three ($|r| \leq 0.38$). The single exception, however, was lichen species richness ($r = -0.68$). More than a quarter of all species were negatively related to this axis. The single strongest positive correlation to axis three was *Cetraria tilesii* ($r = 0.59$). Although far more weakly related, *Solorina bispora*, *Dactylina beringica*, *Cladonia pocillum* and *Coelocaulon muricatum* ($0.35 \leq r \leq 0.30$) were also positively associated with axis three. Lichens most negatively associated with this axis, ordered by decreasing strength, included *Cladonia coccifera*, *Cladina stygia* and *Cladonia gracilis* ssp. *elongata*; yet, an additional 20 species also had strong negative correlations ($r \geq -0.40$) to this axis.

Park Differences

Lichen community composition among parks differed significantly (MRPP; $p < 0.001$, $A = 0.08$). Moreover, all pairwise comparisons between park units significantly differed in community composition (MRPP; all $p \leq 0.02$; Table 6). The effect size of these differences, or the A-statistics, however, showed some parks differed more than others (Table 6). BELA appeared to be the most compositionally distinct of the four compared park units (all $A \geq 0.05$; Table 6). The low A-statistics between all other units (CAKR, KOVA and NOAT) indicate small differences in lichen community composition. The statistical significance associated with these minor differences may also be skewed by large sample sizes (McCune and Grace 2002).

Table 6. Pairwise comparisons in lichen community composition among parks using MRPP. Effect sizes of each comparison (chance-corrected within-group agreement; A-statistics) appear in the upper right, and p-values of each difference appear in the lower left.

	BELA	CAKR	KOVA	NOAT
BELA		$A = 0.05$	$A = 0.07$	$A = 0.06$
CAKR	$p < 0.01$		$A = 0.01$	$A = 0.02$
KOVA	$p < 0.01$	$p = 0.02$		$A = 0.04$
NOAT	$p < 0.01$	$p < 0.01$	$p < 0.01$	

In addition, BELA was distinct from all other ARCN park units based on the other measured environmental variables. BELA had the lowest duff, rock, tree, shrub, subshrub and bryophyte cover, yet the greatest water and graminoid cover (Table 3). Sampled areas within BELA had flatter slopes (Table 3), and were underlain by more silicate bedrock and acidic substrates than any other park unit. Lichen communities within BELA had the lowest species diversity, greatest cover, and were represented by the latest successional communities (Table 3).

Discussion

Elevation-Moisture Gradient

Ordinations based on lichen species composition within ARCN reveal a gradient that combines elevation and moisture along the second, strongest axis. Along this axis, lowland, wet sites dominated by graminoids and shrubs (high axis 2 scores) grade into higher elevation sites that are dry, steep and rocky (low axis 2 scores). Lichens occupying the lowland end of this axis often are more tolerant of mossy, acidic settings, including various species of *Cladina* and *Cladonia*. Due to low elevations and relative topographic position, these areas often accumulate organic material causing acidification (Fenton et al. 2005; Holt et al. 2007). *Sphagnum*, other bryophytes and vascular plants rapidly colonize such areas, due to their geologic stability and high moisture availability.

Permafrost of varying depths and continuity underlie most of northwestern Alaska (Jorgenson et al. 2008). Lowlands, as found at the positive end of axis two, tend to have continuous permafrost, maintained by the overlying layer of organic material (Holt et al. 2009). Flat topography that characterizes these sites promotes continual saturation of the soil despite seasonal melting (Van Patten 1990). Conversely, higher elevations either have thick active layers with better drainage due to the sloped nature of these landscapes (Van Patten 1990), or their soil profiles are shallow, situating permafrost near the surface, thus do not remain frozen during the summer. The resulting dry uplands support less cover of vascular plants for lack of available moisture and deep soils (Holt et al. 2009).

Alpine habitats in northwestern Alaska occur on steep, rocky mountain tops at high elevations; slope, rockiness and elevation are all intercorrelated ($r \geq 0.60$) within ARCN. Although vascular plants are sparse, lichens thrive in these dry, alpine areas. Species such as *Cetraria nivalis*, *C. tilesii*, *Thamnolia subuliformis*, *Dactylina ramulosa*, *Alectoria ochroleuca* and *Asahinea chrysantha* are adapted to alpine environments exemplified by high wind and solar radiation exposure (Rikkinen 1995; Holt et al. 2009). Moreover, the strongest environmental factor correlated to axis two is rock cover; thus alpine sites are rockier than lowland sites.

A similar gradient contrasting alpine communities to moist tundra environments was found in a separate study from plots only within NOAT (Holt et al. 2009). Likewise, an independent study of strictly BELA plots demonstrated strong patterns of topography and rockiness (Holt et al. 2007). These similarities highlight the importance of this elevation-moisture gradient in Arctic lichen community composition, regardless of spatial scale (i.e., individual park units or all of ARCN).

Substrate Gradient

The third ordination axis represents a gradient in substrate chemistry. The positive end of this gradient is dominated by calciphiles, while the negative end is occupied by acidophiles. Substrate pH can greatly influence the composition of the overlying flora, including both epiphytic and terricolous lichens (e.g., Robinson et al. 1989; Kuusinen 1996; Kermit and Gauslaa 2001; Holt et al. 2007; Holt et al. 2009). ARCN hosts a patchwork of calcareous and noncalcareous bedrock types (Beikman 1980; Moore et al. 1994). Within BELA, approximately 24% of plots were underlain by calcareous bedrock, 59% in CAKR, 73% in NOAT and 82% in KOVA (Beikman 1980).

This community gradient contrasting calciphilic macrolichens with acidophiles does not, however, reflect a simple pattern of differences in underlying bedrock. In fact, overlays of bedrock type depict plots underlain by calcareous substrates at both the positive and negative ends of axis three (Fig 3). To unravel the complexity of this substrate gradient, interpretation must concurrently consider patterns associated with the second ordination axis, the elevation-moisture gradient. At the wet, lowland end of axis two, bedrock type lends no extra insight into explaining lichen community patterns, as calcareous and acidic plots mix at both ends of axis three (Fig. 3; small symbols). This lack of pattern is not surprising as lowland sites are more susceptible to paludification, and accumulated water and organic matter may form a barrier between the chemistry of bedrock and rootless lichens above. Moreover, *Sphagnum* that colonizes and sometimes dominates these sites has a high cation exchange capacity thereby increasing the acidity of its surrounding environment (Clymo 1964; Andrus 1986), regardless of underlying bedrock type.

On the contrary, alpine plots at the opposing end of axis two obviously separate by bedrock type (Fig. 3; large symbols). Rocky, alpine sites underlain by calcareous bedrock cluster at the positive end of axis three while similar exposed sites over acidic bedrock cluster at the negative end of this gradient. Alpine areas within ARCN are characterized by high rock and bare soil cover. The paucity of vegetation minimizes organic debris, which may otherwise buffer lichens from the influence of bedrock chemistry as evident in the lowland sites. Instead alpine sites, with their thin soils and little to no organic horizons, directly expose terricolous lichens to bedrock chemistry which largely determines community composition on these sites.

Lichen species richness was the single strongest factor associated with the substrate gradient. Calciphilic communities tended to be lower in diversity, while their counterpart acid-loving communities were more speciose. Similarly, Gould and Walker (1999) found minor but significant negative correlations of lichen species richness and soil pH. These patterns both contrast with previous findings of higher vascular plant diversity with increasing substrate pH in similar environments (Gough et al. 2000; Pärtel 2002). Our relationship between lichen species richness and substrate chemistry, however, was only evident in multivariate analyses. Univariate comparisons of bedrock type showed almost no difference in richness between calcareous and silicate substrates (mean richness = 28.8 and 28.1, respectively; $p = 0.66$ in ANOVA). The mechanism explaining our observed negative relationship between lichen diversity and substrate pH is unclear.

Possibly the calcareous substrate imposes chemical constraints on organisms inhabiting these habitats. Only species adapted to these conditions, determined by environmental tolerances and distribution, are capable of inhabiting such substrates. For example, many of the calcareous-affiliated lichen taxa, including *Cetraria tilesii*, *Solorina bispora*, *Dactylina beringica* and *Cladonia pocillum*, are obligate calciphiles (Hope-Simpson 1941; Thomson 1984; Holt et al. 2009). Their specialized physiological adaptation to this unique habitat may represent an evolutionary advantage, allowing these species to be superior competitors thereby reducing their local community diversity. Although the underlying driver for our observed pattern of increased diversity on acidic substrates is unknown, this gradient in lichen community composition is undeniably clear.

BELA v. Other Park Units

Geographically, BELA is the most isolated park unit located in the far southwestern portion of ARCN (Fig. 1). It is the only park unit on the Seward Peninsula, while all four others are part of the mountains or lowlands of the Brooks Range. This spatial segregation manifests as a distinct geologic and biologic disparity.

BELA is less dominated by woody vascular plants and bryophytes than the other ARCN park units. Its landscapes are primarily comprised of flat, wet tundra occupied by graminoids and lichens. The relative lack of topography in BELA inhibits drainage of seasonal active layer melt, while cool summer temperatures additionally exclude trees. *Eriophorum* and *Carex* blanket moist lowland habitats that extend through most of the preserve, and lichens able to tolerate the competition grow tall and flourish (Holt et al. 2007). Wetlands or extremely wet, lowland tundra habitats which cannot support successful lichen communities do exist in BELA, but were avoided in our sampling. This sampling disparity may partially account for the biological distinction between BELA and all other ARCN units; yet, reduced vascular competition obviously also greatly influences the non-vascular flora.

In addition, BELA houses minimal calcareous substrates in contrast to all other ARCN park units. Most rocky areas within BELA contain silicate rocks, providing ideal conditions for lichens by minimizing vascular competition yet not invoking too harsh of habitats to inhibit lichen growth. Cover of lichens within these rocky BELA sites was on average over 50% (Holt et al. 2007). Undoubtedly, these rocky plots contributed to BELA attaining the greatest lichen cover of all ARCN parks. Despite this massive coverlet of lichens, however, BELA showed the lowest lichen species diversity of all park units. The explanation for this pattern lies in BELA's exceptionally high successional scores, indicating late-successional lichen communities. Late-successional species characteristically cannot tolerate intense or frequent disturbance, yet often dominate stable habitats. Rocky, acidic sites in BELA—found in the lava beds and granitic slopes of the Bendelebens—epitomize these stable habitats.

In sum, lichen community composition within BELA is clearly distinct from all other ARCN park units. The first ordination axis separates BELA plots from all other parks (Fig. 3). Likewise, pairwise comparisons of lichen community composition between park units, highlights BELA as the most dissimilar (Table 6). Reduced vascular competition and its lack of epiphytic and calcareous surfaces create the different environment that is BELA.

Conclusions

Twelve years of lichen sampling within ARCN has provided a thorough baseline of the communities present within its five park units. We found 491 unique lichen taxa (71% of which were macrolichens) from 445 plots or surveys. Our purpose with this sampling effort was to understand the macrolichen diversity within ARCN. Jackknife estimates adjust macrolichen gamma diversity to 416 or 449 species, depending on the estimator. Although this is a tremendous storehouse of information, it represents only a fragment of the total non-vascular flora. The 138 microlichen species discovered incidentally in the opportunistic surveys and 20 plots within NOAT provide a tiny glimpse into the microlichen flora, which if accounted for might double or more the observed gamma diversity for ARCN (B. McCune, pers. comm.). Furthermore, no thorough bryophyte inventories have been conducted within these five parks, and are the next obvious step for ARCN inventory efforts.

Our summary of lichen taxa and description of ARCN-wide lichen community structure and its relation to environment provides a snapshot of macrolichen communities in Arctic Alaska for future comparisons. For example, ARCN is actively used by several caribou herds, including Alaska's largest herd, the Western Arctic Herd (Dau 2000). In addition, reindeer have been managed on the Seward Peninsula for the past hundred years (Postell 1990). Both these animals use lichens for winter forage (Scotter 1967; White and Trudell 1980; Heggberget et al. 2002). Extensive research shows that consumption and trampling by these ungulates can reduce lichen biomass (Gilbert 1974), relative abundance (Helle and Aspi 1983) and growth and community composition (Holt et al. 2008). Our current estimates of diversity, distribution and community patterns can be used for long-term monitoring within ARCN to assess how its lichen communities respond to future levels of grazing by native and managed ungulates.

Furthermore, future climate scenarios forecast Arctic environments will be drastically different from current ecosystems. Global warming has been unequivocally correlated to poleward and elevational shifts in species range distributions (IPCC 2007). These shifts carry large ecological consequences for lichen communities in Arctic environments, which have limited habitats above them (in a latitudinal and elevational context) towards which to move. Areas within ARCN that currently support prolific and diverse lichen communities as evidenced by our present study will likely become more favorable for vascular plants. Advancing trees, shrubs and forbs can replace the non-vascular tundra flora, greatly diminishing their abundance and diversity (Walker et al. 2006). Such a pattern has already been demonstrated on the Seward Peninsula, just south of ARCN, with black spruce encroachment (Lloyd et al. 2003). Alternatively, woodland floor and epiphytic lichens, not currently dominant in ARCN, may benefit from such a transition. The future state of ARCN's lichen communities, therefore, may more closely resemble the mixed forest-alpine communities of southern or interior Alaska, not the communities documented in the current work.

Global climate change is likely to deepen the active layer and produce local thermokarst features (Gorham 1995). As noted above, increasing active layer depth often decreases shallow water impoundment, allowing for shrub and tree colonization of previously lichen-rich tundra habitats. In other localized instances, mesic to wet lichen tussock tundra induced by poor drainage may become wet fens on the edges of newly created thermokarst ponds, creating habitats far too moist for lichens to survive (Gorham 1995). In either situation, warming, which increases the depth of permafrost, is likely to reduce tundra lichen habitats within ARCN. Additionally, fire frequency and severity has also been positively related to warmer, drier environments (Johnson and Larsen 1991; Kasischke et al. 1995). Holt and others (2008) found tundra fires near ARCN decrease lichen abundance and diversity. In sum, as the Arctic continues to warm and fires increase, tundra lichens may be negatively impacted.

Recommendations

The present study not only contributes to our understanding of some lesser known components of ARCN's flora, but also provides an extensive network of 445 sample units which represent an ideal framework for long-term monitoring needed in these ecosystems. This plot network offers ARCN the opportunity to assess how grazing, climate change and air pollution will affect lichen communities. Monitoring may reveal changes in lichen community composition, diversity, growth and abundance attributable to direct or indirect anthropogenic activities.

ARCN has numerous vital signs that would benefit from continued monitoring of these lichen plots: Terrestrial Vegetation and Soils, Wet and Dry Deposition, Caribou, Muskox, Fire Extent and Severity, and Weather and Climate (Lawler et al. 2009). Ideally monitoring data would be gathered once per decade from each of these plots; however, the high logistical and financial expense likely allows sampling of only a subset of this plot network. Holt and others (2008) were able to observe general temporal trends of lichen community composition following fires using only eight plots, yet all sites were located within about 50 km of one another. Variation in lichen community composition across the much larger ARCN is very high (Table 3; β-diversity = 10.2), and roughly 75 plots are needed to capture the maximum species richness (Figure 2). An intermediate number of plots (~50) within a narrower range of habitats (i.e., a subset of vegetation strata of interest, such as lichen-dominated or especially speciose strata) could minimize this variability and reduce logistical and financial costs.

A rotating panel design, or revisiting a subset of these plots each year until all plots are visited, performs well for status and trend detection (Urquhart et al. 1998). Ideally, we recommend using this sampling design with a large fraction of our 249 plots used in the gradient analysis, all of which share similar sampling methods. A multi-year rotation would enable visitation of a manageable number of plots (~30) each year. Due to the relatively pristine conditions within ARCN, including slow average fire cycles, minimal development and recently reduced reindeer husbandry (Holt et al. 2008), this multi-year rotating panel design may be successfully implemented with a several year rest period between cycles.

We therefore make the following specific recommendations:

1. Our lichen plots or a subset thereof should be included in ARCN's monitoring program under the Terrestrial Vegetation and Soils vital sign, but with established linkages to other vital signs.
2. Vascular plant data via point intercept methods of standard ARCN vegetation plots should be added, and vascular relevé data should be added for all plants ≥1% cover.

3. Bryophyte community data should be monitored using the same methlogy within a subset of our plots to create a set of master biodiversity monitoring plots. These plots will complement ARCN's vegetation plots that are designed to capture gross changes in community structure.
4. The proposed grazing exclosures in BELA should be coupled wherever possible with existing lichen plots.
5. NRCS grazing class evaluations should be conducted at all plots to assign a damage class to each plot.
6. A new height measurement method based on Moen (2007) should be applied to existing plots. Each plot should then be back-calibrated using formulas comparing heights derived by pulling lichen strands out of the tundra versus those those derived by measuring them in situ with a push rod.

The large lichen plots of this study complement ARCN's Terrestrial Vegetation and Soils plots for several reasons. First, ARCN's vegetation plots have been designed to capture basic information on growth form and physical structure without capturing detailed information on biodiversity. Their prime objective is to capture basic attributes quickly and link these to remote sensing products for network-wide inference on gross vegetation change. Since anthropogenic changes (e.g., climate change, pollution, grazing) may influence diversity, this lichen plot network could provide the detailed community and species-level data intentionally absent in ARCN's vegetation plots. Second, lichen plots could easily be surveyed for more detailed species-level information on bryophytes and vasculars, thus serving as primary community-level biodiversity plot in the network. Third, the large size of these lichen plots can maximize species capture not possible on smaller vegetation point-count plots. A subset of these lichen plots will be remeasured as part of the Terrestrial Vegetation and Soils vital sign in BELA in order to monitor ungulate grazing effects and will complement the grazing exclosures being erected to serve as a calibration data set for winter range. Converting height measurement methods of plots to that based on Moen (2007) will not only allow for biomass estimation, but will allow us to interface with the large network of lichen-fire-grazing plots (Joly 2007, 2009) on adjacent land ownerships (BLM, USFWS) for a broader scale of inference relevant to the movements of large herds of ungulates.

Literature Cited

Ahti, T. 1959. Studies on the caribou lichen stands of Newfoundland. Annales Botanici Societatis Zoologicae Botanicae Fennicae Vanamo **30**: 1-44.

Ahti, T. 1998. A revision of *Cladonia stricta*. Folia Cryptogamica Estonica, Fasc. **32**: 5-8.

Andrus, R. E. 1986. Some aspects of *Sphagnum* ecology. Canadian Journal of Botany **64**: 416-426.

Anisimov, O. A., D. G. Vaughan, T. V. Callaghan, C. Furgal, H. Marchant, T. D. Prowse, H. Vilhjálmsson, and J. E. Walsh. 2007. Polar regions (Arctic and Antarctic). Pages 653-685 *in* M. L. Parry, O. F. Canziani, J. P. Palutikof, P. J. van der Linden, and C. E. Hanson, editors, Climate Change 2007: Impacts, Adaptation and Vulnerability. Contribution of Working Group II to the Fourth Assessment Report of the Intergovernmental Panel on Climate Change. Cambridge University Press, Cambridge, UK.

Bachelet, D., J. Lenihan, R. Neilson, R. Drapek, and T. Kittel. 2005. Simulating the response of natural ecosystems and their fire regimes to climatic variability in Alaska. Canadian Journal of Forest Research **35**: 2244-2257.

Beikman, H. M. 1980. Geologic map of Alaska: U.S. Geological Survey Special Map, Map SG0002-1T and 2T (scale 1:2,500,000). Available at: http://agdc.usgs.gov/data/usgs/geology/metadata/beikman.html. Accessed 12 March 2009.

Berryman, S., A. Rosso, and P. Neitlich. 2010. Lichen Inventory of Kobuk Valley National Park and Cape Krusenstern National Monument. Unpublished Report in preparation.

Brodo, I., S. D. Sharnoff, and S. Sharnoff. 2001. Lichens of North America. Yale University Press, New Haven, CT, US.

Burnham, K. P. and W. S. Overton. 1979. Robust estimation of population size when capture probabilities vary among animals. Ecology **60**:927-936.

Clymo, R. S. 1964. The origin of acidity in *Sphagnum* bogs. Bryologist **67**: 427 431.

Cornelissen, J. H. C., P. M. van Bodegom, R. Aerts, T. V. Callaghan, R. S. P. van Logtestijn, J. Alatalo, F. S. Chapin, R. Gerdol, J. Gudmundsson, D. Gwynn-Jones, and others. 2007. Global negative vegetation feedback to climate warming responses of leaf litter decomposition rates in cold biomes. Ecology Letters **10**: 1-9.

Daly, C. 2002a. Alaska average monthly or annual mean temperature, 1961-90. (Raster spatial data layers). Spatial Climate Analysis Service at Oregon State University (SCAS/OSU), Corvallis, OR. Distributed by ClimateSource, Inc.

Daly, C. 2002b. Alaska average monthly or annual precipitation, 1961-90. (Raster spatial data layers). Spatial Climate Analysis Service at Oregon State University (SCAS/OSU), Corvallis, OR. Distributed by ClimateSource, Inc.

Dau, J. 2000. Managing reindeer and wildlife on Alaska's Seward Peninsula. Polar Research **19**: 57-62.

Edwards, M. E., T. D. Hamilton, S. A. Elias, N. H. Bigelow, and A. P. Krumhardt. 2003. Interglacial extension of the boreal forest limit in the Noatak Valley, Northwest Alaska: Evidence from an exhumed river-cut bluff and debris apron. Arctic Antarctic and Alpine Research **35**: 460-468.

Esslinger, T. L. 2008. A cumulative checklist for the lichen-forming, lichenicolous and allied fungi of the continental United States and Canada. Version 14, North Dakota State University, Fargo, ND, US. Available at:

http://www.ndsu.nodak.edu/instruct/esslinge/chcklst/chcklst7.htm. Accessed 21 June 2009.

Fenton, N., N. Lecomte, S. Légaré, and Y. Bergeron. 2005. Paludification in black spruce (*Picea mariana*) forests of eastern Canada: Potential factors and management implications. Forest Ecology and Management **213**: 151-159.

Gilbert, O. L. 1974. Reindeer grazing in Britain. Lichenologist **6**: 165-167.

Gorham, E. 1995. The biogeography of northern peatlands and its possible responses to global warming. Pages 169-187 *in* G. M. Woodwell and F. T. Mackenzie, editors. Biotic Feedbacks in the Global Climatic System: Will the Warming feed the Warming? Oxford University Press, US.

Gough, L., G. S. Shaver, J. Carroll, D. L. Royer, and J. A. Laundre. 2000. Vascular plant species richness in Alaskan arctic tundra: the importance of soil pH. Journal of Ecology **88**: 54-66.

Gould, W. A. and M. D. Walker. 1999. Plant communities and landscape diversity along a Canadian Artic River. Journal of Vegetation Science **10**: 537-548.

Goward, T. 1999. The Lichens of British Columbia. Part II—Fruticose Species. Ministry of the Forests, Research Program, Victoria, BC.

Goward, T., O. Bruess, B. Ryan, B. McCune, H. Sipman, and C. Scheidegger. 1996. Notes on the lichens and allied fungi of British Columbia. III. Bryologist **99**: 439-449.

Goward, T., B. McCune, and D. Meidinger. 1994. The Lichens of British Columbia. Part I—Foliose and Squamulose Species. Ministry of the Forests, Research Program, Victoria, BC.

Gunther, A. J. 1989. Nitrogen fixation by lichens in a subarctic Alaskan watershed. The Bryologist **92**: 202-208.

Hamilton, T.D. 2009. Guide to surficial geology and river-bluff exposures, Noatak National Preserve, northwestern Alaska. US Department of Interior and US Geologic Survey. USGS Scientific Investigations Report 2008-5125.

Heggberget, T. M., E. Gaare, and J. P. Ball. 2002. Reindeer (*Rangifer tarandus*) and climate change: importance of winter forage. Rangifer **22**: 13-32.

Helle, T. and J. Aspi. 1983. Effects of winter grazing by reindeer on vegetation. Oikos **40**: 337-343.

Heltshe, J. F. and N. E. Forrester. 1983. Estimating species richness using the jackknife procedure. Biometrics **39**:1-12.

Hobara, S., C. McCalley, K. Koba, A. E. Giblin, M. S. Weiss, G. M. Gettel, and G. R. Shaver. 2006. Nitrogen fixation in surface soils and vegetation in an arctic tundra watershed: A key source of atmospheric nitrogen. Arctic Antarctic and Alpine Research **38**: 363-372.

Holt, E. A., B. McCune, and P. Neitlich. 2006. Defining a successional metric for lichen communities in the arctic tundra. Arctic Antarctic and Alpine Research **38**: 373-377.

Holt, E. A., B. McCune, and P. Neitlich. 2007. Succession and community gradients of Arctic macrolichens and their relation to substrate, topography, and rockiness. Pacific Northwest Fungi **2**: 1-21.

Holt, E. A., B. McCune, and P. Neitlich. 2008. Grazing and fire impacts on macrolichen communities of the Seward Peninsula, Alaska, USA. The Bryologist **111**: 68-83.

Holt, E. A., B. McCune, and P. Neitlich. 2009. Macrolichen communities in relation to soils and vegetation in the Noatak National Preserve, Alaska. Botany **87**: 241-252.

Hope-Simpson, J. F. 1941. Studies of the vegetation of the English chalk: VII. Bryophytes and lichens in chalk grasslands, with a comparison of their occurrence in other calcareous grasslands. Journal of Ecology **29**: 107-116.

Hutchinson, J. And B. McCune. 2001. Riparian lichens of Northern Idaho. Idaho Bureau of Land Management, Technical Bulletin No. 01-12.

Ihl, C. and D. R. Klein. 2001. Habitat and diet selection by muskoxen and reindeer in western Alaska. Journal of Wildlife Management **65**: 964-972.

Jorgenson, M. T., J. E. Roth, M. Emers, W. Davis, S. F. Schlentner, and M. J. Macander. 2004. Landcover mapping for Bering Land Bridge National Preserve and Cape Krusenstern National Monument, Northwestern Alaska. ABR, Inc. Environmental Research and Services, Fairbanks, AK, US.

Jorgenson T., M. Kanevskiy, Y. Shur, V. Romanovsky, S. Marchenko, G. Grosse, J. Brown, and B. Jones. 2008. Permafrost characteristics of Alaska. Institute of Northern Engineering, Scale 1:7,200,000. University of Alaska, Fairbanks, AK, US.

Kermit, T. and Y. Gauslaa. 2001. The vertical gradient of bark pH of twigs and macrolichens in a *Picea abies* canopy not affected by acid rain. Lichenologist **33**: 353-359.

Kruskal, J. B. 1964. Nonmetric multidimensional scaling: a numerical method. Psychometrika **29**: 115-129.

Kuusinen, M. 1996. Epiphyte flora and diversity on basal trunks of six old-growth forest tree species in southern and middle boreal Finland. Lichenologist **28**: 443-463.

Lamb, I. M. 1977. A conspectus of the lichen genus *Stereocaulon* (Schreb.) Hoffm. Journal of the Hattori Botanical Laboratory **43**: 191-355.

Lawler, J. P., J. Ver Hoef, and S. B. Young. 2009. Arctic network vital signs monitoring plan. US Department of Interior, National Park Service. Natural Resources Report NPS/ARCN/NRR-2009/088. Fort Collins, CO, US.

Lindblom, L and U. Søchting. 2008. Taxonomic revision of *Xanthomendoza borealis* and *Xanthoria mawsonii* (Lecanoromycetes, Ascomycota). Lichenologist **40**: 399-409

Lloyd, A. H., T. S. Rupp, C. L. Fastie, and A.M. Starfield. 2003: Patterns and dynamics of treeline advance on the Seward Peninsula,Alaska. Journal of Geophysical Research **108**: 8161.

Manley, W. F., and C. Daly. 2005. Alaska Geospatial Climate Animations of Monthly Temperature and Precipitation: INSTAAR, University of Colorado. Available at: (http://instaar.colorado.edu/QGISL/AGCA). Accessed 9 April 2009.

Markon, C. J. and S. D. Wesser. 1997. The Bering Land Bridge National Preserve Land Cover Map and its Comparability with 1995 Field Conditions. US Geological Survey Open File Report 97-103, Anchorage, AK, US.

Markon, C. J. and S. D. Wesser. 1998. The Northwest Alaskan parks land cover map. Open File Report 00-51, US Geological Survey. National Park Service, Alaska Regional Office, Anchorage, AK, US. Available at: http://science.nature.nps.gov/nrdata. Accessed 17 December 2005.

Mather, P. M. 1976. Computation methods of multivariate analysis in physical geography. J. Wiley and Sons, London, UK.

McCune, B. 2000. Lichen communities as indicators of forest health. The Bryologist **103**: 353-356.

McCune, B. 2008. Three new species of *Hypogymnia* (Ascomycota: Parmeliaceae) from the Bering Sea region, Alaska and Russia. North American Fungi **3**: 1-10.

McCune, B. and J. B. Grace. 2002. Analysis of Ecological Communities. MjM Software, Gleneden Beach, OR, US.

McCune, B. and D. Keon. 2002. Equations for potential annual direct incident radiation and heat load. Journal of Vegetation Science **13**: 603-606.

McCune, B. and M. J. Mefford. 2005. Multivariate analysis on the PC-ORD system. Version 5. MjM Software, Gleneden Beach, OR, US.

McCune, B., J. P. Dey, J. E. Peck, D. Cassell, K. Heiman, S. Will-Wolf, and P. N. Neitlich. 1997. Repeatability of community data: species richness versus gradient scores in large-scale lichen studies. The Bryologist **100**: 40-46.

McCune, B., E. A. Holt, P. Neitlich, T. Ahti, R. Rosentreter. 2009. Macrolichen diversity in Noatak National Preserve, Alaska. North American Fungi **4**: 1-22.

Milner, A. M., M. W. Oswood, and K. R. Munkittrick. 2005. Rivers of Arctic North America. Pages 903-938 *in* A. C. Benke and C. E. Cushing, editors. Rivers of North America. Elsevier Academic Press, Amsterdam, NL.

Moen, J., Ö. Danell, and R. Holt. 2007. Non-destructive estimation of lichen biomass. Rangifer **27**: 41-46.

Moore, T. E., W. K. Wallace, K. J. Bird, S. M. Karl, C. G. Mull, and J. T. Dillon. 1994. Geology of northern Alaska. Pages 49-140 *in* G. Plafker and H. C. Berg, editors.The geology of Alaska. Geological Society of America, The Geology of North America, v G-1. Boulder, CO, US.

National Park Service. 2010. AlaskaPak Toolkit for ArcGIS, v. 2.2. National Park Service, GIS Team, 240 W 5th Ave, Anchorage, AK 99501. Available at: http://science.nature.nps.gov/nrgis/applications/gisapps/gis_tools/8x/alaskapak.aspx. Accessed 20 May 2010.

Neitlich, P. N. and L. M. Hasselbach. 1998. Lichen inventory and status assessment for Gates of the Arctic National Park, Alaska. NPS General Technical Report, Fairbanks, AK, US.

Neitlich, P., S. Berryman, A. Mines, and J. VerHoef. 2010. Effects of heavy metal-enriched road dust from the Red Dog Mine haul road on tundra vegetation in Cape Krusenstern National Monument, Alaska. In prep.

NPLichen. 2009. A Database of Lichens in the US National Parks. Version 4.5, US Geological Survey. Available at: http://www.ies.wisc.edu/nplichen. Accessed 21 June 2009.

Palmer, M. W. 1990. The estimation of species richness by extrapolation. Ecology **71**:1195-1198.

Palmer, M. W. 1991. Estimating species richness: the second-order jackknife reconsidered. Ecology **72**:1512-1513.

Palmer, M. W. 1995. How should one count species? Natural Areas Journal **15**:124-135.

Panarctic Lichen Checklist. 2006. Database compiled by CAFF-Flora group. Available at: http://archive.arcticportal.org/276/01/Panarctic_lichen_checklist.pdf. Accessed 28 June 2009.

Pärtel, M. 2002. Local plant diversity patterns and evolutionary history at the regional scale. Ecology **83**: 2361-2366.

Péwé, T. L. 1975. Quaternary geology of Alaska. US Geologic Survey. Geological Survey Professional Paper 835. US Government Printing Office, Washington, US.

Postell, A. 1990. Where Did the Reindeer Come From? Amaknak Press, Portland, OR, US.

Rikkinen, J. 1995. What's behind the pretty colors? A study on the photobiology of lichens. Bryobrothera **4**: 3-239.

Robinson, A. L., D. H. Vitt, and K. P. Timoney. 1989. Patterns of community structure and morphology of bryophytes and lichens relative to edaphic gradients in the subarctic forest-tundra of northwestern Canada. The Bryologist **92**: 495-512.

Sokal, R. R. and F. J. Rohlf. 1995. Biometry: the principals and practices of statistics in biological research. 3rd edition. W.H. Freeman and Company, New York, NY, US

Steen, E. 1965. Reindeer grazing problems. Acta Phytogeographa Suecica **50**: 281-284.

Scotter, G. W. 1964. Effects of forest fires on the winter range of barren-ground caribou in Northern Saskatchewan. Wildlife Management Bulletin **18**: 1-86.

Scotter, G. W. 1967. The winter diet of barren-ground caribou in northern Canada. Canadian Field Naturalist **81**: 33-39.

Swanson, D. and P. Spencer. 2001. Ecological, Subsections, Ecoregions, National Park, Kobuk Valley. GIS data layer available from: GIS Team, National Park Service, 240 W 5th Ave., Anchorage, AK 99501. Available at: http://science.nature.nps.gov/nrdata/. Accessed 20 May 2010.

Thomson, J. W. 1984. American Arctic Lichens. I. The Macrolichens. Columbia University Press, New York, NY, US.

Thomson, J. W. 1998. American Arctic Lichens II. The Microlichens. University of Wisconsin Press, Madison, WI, US.

Urquhart, N. S., S. G. Paulsen, and D. P. Larsen. 1998. Monitoring for policy-relevant regional trends over time. Ecological Applications **8**: 246-257.

USDA, NRCS. 2009. The PLANTS Database. National Plant Data Center, Baton Rouge, LA, US. Available at: http://plants.usda.gov. Accessed 21 June 2009.

Van Patten, D. J. 1990. Soil Investigation of Seward Peninsula area, Alaska. USDA-Natural Resource Conservation Service in cooperation with Reindeer Herders Association, OCLC No. ocm36843275, Palmer, AK, US.

Viereck, L. A., C. T. Dyrness, A. R. Batten, and K. J. Wenzlick. 1992. The Alaska Vegetation Classification. USDA-Forest Service PNW-General Technical Report 286, Portland, OR, US.

Walker, M. D., C. H. Wahren, R. D. Hollister, G. H. R. Henry, L. E. Ahlquist, J. M. Alatalo, M. S. Bret-Harte, M. P. Calef, T. V. Callaghan, A. B. Carroll, and others. 2003. Plant community responses to experimental warming across the tundra biome. Proceedings of the National Academy of Sciences **103**: 1342-1346.

Westberg, M., I. Kärnefelt, and A. Thell. 2004. *Melanelia agnate*, an overlooked species, new to Sweden. Graphis Scripta **16**: 23-27.

White, R. G. and J. Trudell. 1980. Habitat preference and forage consumption of reindeer and caribou near Alkasook, Alaska. Arctic and Alpine Research **12**: 511-529.

Whittaker, R. H. 1972. Evolution and measurement of species diversity. Taxon **21**: 213-251.

Appendix 1. Lichen species list from 445 sites within ARCN, including 351 macrolichens, 138 microlichens and 2 basidiolichens.

Species	Code	Freq	Within Park Frequency (% plots)					Rarity	Form
			BELA	CAKR	GAAR	KOVA	NOAT		
Alectoria nigricans (Ach.) Nyl.	Alenig	105	60	13	11	24	11	C	M
Alectoria ochroleuca (Hoffm.) A. Massal.	Aleoch	118	51	16	11	39	22	C	M
Allantoparmelia almquistii (Vainio) Essl.	Allalm	19	1	0	21	11	1	O	M
Allantoparmelia alpicola (Th. Fr.) Essl.	Allalp	11	0	1	2	18	1	U	M
Anaptychia bryorum Poelt	Anabry	1	0	0	2	0	0	U	M
Anaptychia ulotrichoides (Vainio) Vainio	Anaulo	1	0	0	2	0	0	U	M
Anzina carneonivea (Anzi) Scheid. (Goward et al. 1996)	Anzcar	1	0	0	0	0	1	U	M
Arctoparmelia centrifuga (L.) Hale	Arccen	31	3	2	21	18	5	O	M
Arctoparmelia incurva (Pers.) Hale	Arcinc	11	0	1	3	16	1	U	M
Arctoparmelia separata (Th. Fr.) Hale	Arcsep	59	16	2	22	21	16	C	M
Arctoparmelia subcentrifuga (Oksner) Hale	Arcsub	1	0	0	0	3	0	U	M
Arthrorhaphis sp. Th. Fr.	Art	1	0	0	0	0	1	U	C
Arthrorhaphis alpina (Schaerer) R. Sant.	Artalp	2	0	0	0	0	2	U	C
Asahinea chrysantha (Tuck.) Culb. & C. Culb.	Asachr	130	40	21	11	42	36	C	M
Asahinea scholanderi (Llano) Culb. & C. Culb.	Asasch	42	14	2	16	16	8	O	M
Aspilidea myrinii (Fr.) Stein	Asdmyr	1	0	0	0	0	1	U	C
Aspicilia sp. A. Massal.	Asp	1	0	0	0	0	1	U	C
Aspicilia caesiopruinosa (H. Magn.) J. W. Thomson	Aspcae	1	0	0	0	0	1	U	C
Aspicilia candida (Anzi) Hue	Aspcan	1	0	0	0	0	1	U	C
Bacidia sp. De Not.	Bac	1	0	0	0	0	1	U	C
Baeomyces carneus Flörke	Baecar	1	0	0	0	0	1	U	C
Baeomyces placophyllus Ach.	Baepla	3	0	0	0	0	3	U	C
Baeomyces rufus (Hudson) Rebent.	Baeruf	4	0	0	0	0	4	U	C
Biatora sp. Fr.	Bia	2	0	0	0	0	2	U	C
Biatora vernalis (L.) Fr.	Biaver	1	0	0	0	0	1	U	C
Bryocaulon divergens (Ach.) Kärnefelt	Brcdiv	143	59	24	14	32	29	C	M
Bryonora sp. Poelt	Brn	1	0	0	0	0	1	U	M
Bryonora castanea (Hepp) Poelt	Brncas	2	0	0	0	0	2	U	C
Brodoa oroarctica (Krog) Goward	Brooro	5	0	0	6	0	1	U	M

Appendix 1. Lichen species list from 445 plots within ARCN, including 351 macrolichens, 138 microlichens and 2 basidiolichens (continued).

Species	Code	Freq	Within Park Frequency (% plots)					Rarity	Form
			BELA	CAKR	GAAR	KOVA	NOAT		
Bryoria sp. Brodo & D. Hawksw.	Bry	6	0	0	6	5	0	U	M
Bryoria species A	BryA	4	0	1	0	8	0	U	M
Bryoria chalybeiformis (L.) Brodo & D. Hawksw.	Brycha	3	2	0	0	3	0	U	M
Bryoria fuscescens (Gyelnik) Brodo & D. Hawksw.	Bryfus	4	1	0	0	0	3	U	M
Bryoria implexa (Hoffm.) Brodo & D. Hawksw.	Bryimp	1	0	0	0	0	1	U	M
Bryoria lanestris (Ach.) Brodo & D. Hawksw.	Brylan	16	0	1	6	11	5	O	M
Bryoria nadvornikiana (Gyelnik) Brodo & D. Hawksw.	Brynad	1	0	0	0	3	0	U	M
Bryoria nitidula (Th. Fr.) Brodo & D. Hawksw.	Brynit	40	19	2	11	8	7	O	M
Bryoria simplicior (Vainio) Brodo & D. Hawksw.	Brysim	18	0	8	2	11	2	O	M
Bryoria trichodes ssp. americana (Mot.) Brodo & D. Hawksw.	Brytra	1	0	0	0	0	1	U	M
Bryoria trichodes ssp. trichodes (Michaux) Brodo & D. Hawksw.	Brytri	6	0	1	0	5	2	U	M
Buellia sp. De Not.	Bue	4	0	0	0	0	4	U	C
Buellia erubescens Arnold	Bueeru	1	0	0	0	0	1	U	C
Buellia notabilis Lynge	Buenot	1	0	0	0	0	1	U	C
Buellia punctata (Hoffm.) A. Massal.	Buepun	1	0	0	0	0	1	U	C
Caloplaca sp. Th. Fr.	Cal	2	0	0	0	0	2	U	C
Caloplaca ammiospila (Wahlenb.) H. Olivier	Calamm	4	0	0	0	0	4	U	C
Caloplaca citrina (Hoffm.) Th. Fr.	Calcit	1	0	0	0	0	1	U	C
Caloplaca holocarpa (Hoffm. ex Ach.) A. E. Wade	Calhol	1	0	0	0	0	1	U	C
Caloplaca jungermanniae (Vahl) Th. Fr.	Caljun	3	0	0	0	0	3	U	C
Caloplaca phaeocarpella (Nyl.) Zahlbr.	Calpha	1	0	0	0	0	1	U	C
Caloplaca saxicola (Hoffm.) Nordin	Calsax	1	0	0	0	0	1	U	C
Caloplaca stillicidiorum (Vahl) Lynge	Calsti	2	0	0	0	0	2	U	C
Caloplaca tetraspora (Nyl.) H. Olivier	Caltet	3	0	0	0	0	3	U	C
Caloplaca tiroliensis Zahlbr.	Caltir	1	0	0	0	0	1	U	C
Candelariella sp. Müll. Arg.	Can	2	0	0	0	0	2	U	C

Appendix 1. Lichen species list from 445 plots within ARCN, including 351 macrolichens, 138 microlichens and 2 basidiolichens (continued).

Species	Code	Freq	Within Park Frequency (% plots)					Rarity	Form
			BELA	CAKR	GAAR	KOVA	NOAT		
Catapyrenium cinereum (Pers.) Körber	Catcin	1	0	0	0	0	1	U	C
Cetrelia alaskana (C. Culb. & Culb.) Culb. & C. Culb.	Celala	7	0	2	0	0	4	U	M
Cetraria sp. Ach.	Cet	3	0	1	0	5	0	U	M
Cetraria andrejevii Oksner	Cetand	10	3	0	3	3	4	U	M
Cetraria commixta (Nyl.) Th.	Cetcom	16	1	1	14	11	1	O	M
Cetraria cucullata (Bellardi) Ach.	Cetcuc	325	92	86	17	82	68	A	M
Cetraria delisei (Bory ex Schaerer) Nyl.	Cetdel	60	13	0	38	16	15	C	M
Cetraria ericetorum Opiz	Ceteri	14	4	0	3	0	7	O	M
Cetraria fastigiata (Delise ex Nyl.) Kärnefelt	Cetfas	4	1	1	0	0	2	U	M
Cetraria halei Culb. & C. Culb.	Cethal	3	0	0	3	3	0	U	M
Cetraria hepatizon (Ach.) Vainio	Cethep	30	5	2	6	34	5	O	M
Cetraria inermis (Nyl.) Krog	Cetine	45	0	24	2	11	6	C	M
Cetraria islandica ssp. crispiformis (Räsänen) Kärnefelt	Cetisc	4	0	0	0	0	4	U	M
Cetraria islandica (L.) Ach.	Cetisl	236	51	57	22	87	56	A	M
Cetraria kamczatica Savicz	Cetkam	47	16	1	8	24	14	C	M
Cetraria laevigata Rass.	Cetlae	267	87	68	11	58	54	A	M
Cetraria nigricans Nyl.	Cetnig	59	16	2	27	24	13	C	M
Cetraria nivalis (L.) Ach.	Cetniv	209	67	29	19	74	58	C	M
Cetraria orbata (Nyl.) Fink	Cetorb	1	0	0	0	0	1	U	M
Cetraria pinastri (Scop.) Gray	Cetpin	159	15	58	6	50	38	C	M
Cetraria sepincola (Ehrh.) Ach.	Cetsep	142	4	66	8	29	29	C	M
Cetraria subalpina Imshaug	Cetsub	1	0	0	0	0	1	U	M
Cetraria tilesii Ach.	Cettil	67	11	4	13	34	27	C	M
Cladonia sp. P. Browne	Cla	40	0	24	3	0	5	O	M
Cladonia acuminata (Ach.) Norrlin	Claacu	19	1	0	5	18	7	O	M
Cladonia alaskana A. Evans	Claala	8	1	1	6	0	2	U	M
Cladonia albonigra Brodo & Ahti (Brodo & Ahti 1996)	Claalb	29	3	7	0	18	8	O	M

Appendix 1. Lichen species list from 445 plots within ARCN, including 351 macrolichens, 138 microlichens and 2 basidiolichens (continued).

Species	Code	Freq	Within Park Frequency (% plots)					Rarity	Form
			BELA	CAKR	GAAR	KOVA	NOAT		
Cladonia amaurocraea (Flörke) Schaerer	Claama	299	80	82	41	53	58	A	M
Cladonia bacillaris Nyl.	Clabac	6	0	0	5	5	1	U	M
Cladonia bacilliformis (Nyl.) Glück	Clabaf	84	22	31	3	26	7	C	M
Cladonia bellidiflora (Ach.) Schaerer	Clabel	83	39	13	10	45	4	C	M
Cladonia borealis S. Stenroos	Clabor	55	9	7	2	34	20	C	M
Cladonia botrytes (K. Hagen) Willd.	Clabot	30	11	1	5	32	2	O	M
Cladonia cariosa (Ach.) Sprengel	Clacai	9	1	0	2	8	4	U	M
Cladonia carneola (Fr.) Fr.	Clacar	47	1	28	10	5	0	C	M
Cladonia cenotea (Ach.) Schaerer	Clacen	83	16	16	8	29	26	C	M
Cladonia cervicornis (Ach.) Flotow	Clacer	24	11	1	2	13	5	O	M
Cladonia chlorophaea (Flörke ex Sommerf.) Sprengel	Clachl	69	6	19	8	21	22	C	M
Cladonia coccifera (L.) Willd.	Clacoc	131	39	33	21	50	14	C	M
Cladonia coniocraea (Flörke) Sprengel	Clacon	34	1	18	3	11	2	O	M
Cladonia cornuta (L.) Hoffm.	Clacor	181	35	65	11	37	34	C	M
Cladonia crispata var. cetrariiformis (Delise) Vainio	Clacrc	3	0	0	0	0	3	U	M
Cladonia crispata (Ach.) Flotow	Clacri	89	17	21	16	37	18	C	M
Cladonia cryptochlorophaea Asah.	Clacry	14	0	2	0	16	5	O	M
Cladonia cyanipes (Sommerf.) Nyl.	Clacya	110	24	30	6	18	31	C	M
Cladonia decorticata (Flörke) Sprengel	Cladec	21	3	6	0	5	7	O	M
Cladonia deformis (L.) Hoffm.	Cladef	74	12	37	2	13	5	C	M
Cladonia digitata (L.) Hoffm.	Cladig	15	3	5	3	3	2	O	M
Cladonia ecmocyna ssp. intermedia (Robbins) Ahti	Claeci	2	0	0	0	5	0	U	M
Cladonia ecmocyna Leighton	Claecm	13	0	4	10	3	1	U	M
Cladonia ecmocyna ssp. occidentalis Ahti (Brodo & Ahti 1996)	Claeco	1	0	0	0	3	0	U	M
Cladonia fimbriata (L.) Fr.	Clafim	109	7	56	6	18	14	C	M
Cladonia furcata (Hudson) Schrader	Clafur	15	5	1	0	5	6	O	M
Cladonia gracilis (no ssp indication) (L.) Willd.	Clagra	72	5	1	24	0	46	C	M

Appendix 1. Lichen species list from 445 plots within ARCN, including 351 macrolichens, 138 microlichens and 2 basidiolichens (continued).

Species	Code	Freq	Within Park Frequency (% plots)					Rarity	Form
			BELA	CAKR	GAAR	KOVA	NOAT		
Cladonia gracilis ssp. elongata (Jacq.) Vainio	Clagre	118	28	49	0	61	2	C	M
Cladonia gracilis spp. gracilis (L.) Willd.	Clagrg	3	0	0	5	0	0	U	M
Cladonia gracilis ssp. turbinata (Ach.) Ahti	Clagrt	60	12	20	10	39	0	C	M
Cladonia gracilis ssp. vulnerata Ahti	Clagrv	28	12	3	0	32	0	O	M
Cladonia grayi G. Merr. ex Sandst.	Clagry	19	6	1	2	13	5	O	M
Cladonia kanewskii Oksner	Clakan	9	0	1	2	5	5	U	M
Cladonia libifera Savicz	Clalib	9	3	0	0	3	5	U	M
Cladonia luteoalba Wheldon & A. Wilson	Clalut	3	0	0	0	0	3	U	M
Cladonia macrophylla (Schaerer) Stenh.	Clamac	50	11	0	19	34	13	C	M
Cladonia macrophyllodes Nyl.	Clamao	4	0	1	3	0	1	U	M
Cladonia macroceras (Delise) Hav.	Clamas	54	13	7	0	37	16	C	M
Cladonia maxima (Asah.) Ahti	Clamax	170	52	59	11	11	25	C	M
Cladonia merochlorophaea Asah.	Clamer	27	2	18	0	0	0	O	M
Cladonia metacorallifera Asah.	Clamet	14	3	4	5	0	3	O	M
Cladonia nipponica Asah.	Clanip	9	7	0	0	0	2	U	M
Cladonia nitens Ahti (Ahti 2007)	Clanit	4	2	0	0	3	1	U	M
Cladonia ochrochlora Flörke	Claoch	68	0	42	3	21	1	C	M
Cladonia phyllophora Hoffm.	Claphy	93	8	40	11	32	10	C	M
Cladonia pleurota (Flörke) Schaerer	Claple	68	10	25	2	29	11	C	M
Cladonia pocillum (Ach.) Grognot	Clapoc	77	7	6	13	45	33	C	M
Cladonia pyxidata (L.) Hoffm.	Clapyx	113	16	28	16	61	23	C	M
Cladonia scabriuscula (Delise) Nyl.	Clasca	38	0	17	3	16	6	O	M
Cladonia scotteri Ahti ined.[1]	Clasco	8	0	0	0	3	6	U	M
Cladonia singularis S. Hammer	Clasin	8	0	1	0	16	0	U	M
Cladonia squamosa Hoffm.	Clasqu	96	14	38	10	37	10	C	M
Cladonia stricta (Nyl.) Nyl.	Clastr	42	4	7	3	21	16	O	M
Cladonia subcervicornis (Vainio) Kernst.	Clasub	1	0	0	2	0	0	U	M
Cladonia subfurcata (Nyl.) Arnold	Clasuf	90	38	15	6	45	11	C	M
Cladonia sulphurina (Michaux) Fr.	Clasul	176	54	49	27	39	23	C	M

36

Appendix 1. Lichen species list from 445 plots within ARCN, including 351 macrolichens, 138 microlichens and 2 basidiolichens (continued).

Species	Code	Freq	Within Park Frequency (% plots)					Rarity	Form
			BELA	CAKR	GAAR	KOVA	NOAT		
Cladonia subulata (L.) F. H. Wigg.	Clasuu	2	0	1	0	3	0	U	M
Cladonia symphycarpa (Ach.) Fr.[1]	Clasya	4	0	0	0	0	4	U	M
Cladonia symphycarpia (Flörke) Fr. (Ahti 2000)[1]	Clasym	4	0	1	0	5	1	U	M
Cladonia thomsonii Ahti	Clatho	3	0	0	2	0	2	U	M
Cladonia trassii Ahti 1998	Clatra	4	0	0	0	0	4	U	M
Cladonia transcendens (Vainio) Vainio	Clatrn	13	0	10	0	0	0	U	M
Cladonia turgida Hoffm.	Clatur	2	0	0	3	0	0	U	M
Cladonia uliginosa (Ahti) Ahti (Ahti 1998)	Clauli	1	0	0	0	0	1	U	M
Cladonia uncialis (L.) F. H. Wigg.	Claunc	194	55	54	17	53	32	C	M
Cladonia verruculosa (Vainio) Ahti	Claver	2	0	0	3	0	0	U	M
Cladonia verticillata (Hoffm.) Schaerer	Clavet	10	0	1	0	13	4	U	M
Cladonia wainioi Savicz	Clawai	12	0	1	6	13	2	U	M
Cladina aberrans (Abbayes) Hale & Culb.	Cldabe	4	0	0	0	0	4	U	M
Cladina arbuscula (Wallr.) Hale & Culb.	Cldarb	204	4	80	19	66	49	C	M
Cladina arbuscula/mitis (isomorphs lumped in field)	Cldarb/m	67	68	0	0	0	0	C	M
Cladina ciliata (Stirton) Trass	Cldcil	5	5	0	0	0	0	U	M
Cladina mitis (Sandst.) Hustich	Cldmit	40	10	3	2	18	16	O	M
Cladina rangiferina (L.) Nyl.	Cldran	216	55	65	17	18	50	C	M
Cladina stellaris (Opiz) Brodo	Cldste	59	24	2	16	34	8	C	M
Cladina stygia (Fr.) Ahti	Cldsty	232	77	69	0	63	35	A	M
Coccocarpia erythroxyli (Sprengel) Swinscow & Krog	Cocery	3	0	0	0	0	3	U	M
Coelocaulon aculeatum (Schreber) Link	Coeacu	9	0	0	8	8	1	U	M
Coelocaulon muricatum (Ach.) J. R. Laundon	Coemur	30	6	1	0	11	16	O	M
Collema sp. F. H. Wigg.	Col	1	0	0	2	0	0	U	M
Collema bachmanianum (Fink) Degel.	Colbac	3	0	0	0	5	1	U	M
Collema callopismum A. Massal.	Colcal	1	0	0	0	0	1	U	M
Collema ceraniscum Nyl.	Colcer	5	0	1	0	8	1	U	M
Collema cristatum (L.) F. H. Wigg.	Colcri	1	0	0	0	0	1	U	M

Appendix 1. Lichen species list from 445 plots within ARCN, including 351 macrolichens, 138 microlichens and 2 basidiolichens (continued).

Species	Code	Freq	Within Park Frequency (% plots)					Rarity	Form
			BELA	CAKR	GAAR	KOVA	NOAT		
Collema curtisporum Degel.	Colcur	3	0	0	0	8	0	U	M
Collema flaccidum (Ach.) Ach.	Colfla	1	0	0	0	3	0	U	M
Collema furfuraceum (Arnold) Du Rietz	Colfur	7	0	1	0	13	1	U	M
Collema fuscovirens (With.) J. R. Laundon	Colfus	20	0	3	0	24	6	O	M
Collema glebulentum (Nyl. ex Crombie) Degel.	Colgle	7	0	1	2	13	0	U	M
Collema multipartitum Sm.	Colmul	1	0	1	0	0	0	U	M
Collema polycarpon Hoffm.	Colpol	5	0	1	0	5	1	U	M
Collema tenax (Sw.) Ach.	Colten	8	0	0	0	0	7	U	M
Collema undulatum Laurer ex Flotow	Colund	3	0	0	0	3	2	U	M
Collema undulatum var. granulosm Degel.	Colung	4	0	0	6	0	0	U	M
Dactylina arctica (Richardson) Nyl.	Dacarc	122	22	24	17	34	40	C	M
Dactylina beringica C. D. Bird & J. W. Thomson	Dacber	47	10	3	0	24	22	C	M
Dactylina madreporiformis (Ach.) Tuck	Dacmad	4	2	0	3	0	0	U	M
Dactylina ramulosa (Hook.) Tuck.	Dacram	76	12	7	21	32	27	C	M
Dibaeis baeomyces (L. f.) Rambold & Hertel	Dibbae	4	0	0	0	3	3	U	C
Diploschistes muscorum ssp. muscorum (Scop.) R. Sant.	Dipmus	2	0	0	0	0	2	U	C
Diploschistes scruposus (Schreber) Norman	Dipscr	1	0	0	0	0	1	U	C
Ephebe hispidula (Ach.) Horwood	Ephhis	1	0	0	0	0	1	U	M
Epilichen scabrosus (Ach.) Clem.	Episca	4	0	0	0	0	4	U	C
Evernia divaricata (L.) Ach.	Evediv	3	0	0	0	0	3	U	M
Evernia mesomorpha Nyl.	Evemes	17	0	1	5	13	6	O	M
Evernia perfragilis Llano	Eveper	18	4	3	0	13	5	O	M
Farnoldia hypocrita (A. Massal.) Frøberg	Farhyp	1	0	0	0	0	1	U	C
Farnoldia jurana (Schaerer) Hertel	Farjur	1	0	0	0	0	1	U	C
Fuscopannaria sp. P. M. Jørg.	Fus	1	0	0	0	0	1	U	C
Fuscopannaria praetermissa (Nyl.) P. M. Jørg.	Fuspra	7	0	1	0	3	5	U	C
Hypogymnia sp. (Nyl.) Nyl.	Hyp	2	1	1	0	0	0	U	M
Hypogymnia austerodes (Nyl.) Räsänen	Hypaus	15	0	3	6	18	0	O	M

Appendix 1. Lichen species list from 445 plots within ARCN, including 351 macrolichens, 138 microlichens and 2 basidiolichens (continued).

Species	Code	Freq	Within Park Frequency (% plots)					Rarity	Form
			BELA	CAKR	GAAR	KOVA	NOAT		
Hypogymnia bitteri (Lynge) Ahti	Hypbit	27	0	1	10	18	11	O	M
Hypogymnia castanea Krog & McCune	Hypcas	2	2	0	0	0	0	U	M
Hypogymnia metaphysodes (Asahina) Rass.	Hypmet	1	0	0	0	3	0	U	M
Hypogymnia physodes (L.) Nyl.	Hypphy	78	11	24	13	26	14	C	M
Hypogymnia subobscura (Vainio) Poelt	Hypsub	72	10	21	14	5	21	C	M
Hypogymnia tubulosa (Schaerer) Hav.	Hyptub	2	0	1	0	0	0	U	M
Hypogymnia vittata (Ach.) Parrique	Hypvit	1	0	0	2	0	0	U	M
Icmadophila ericetorum (L.) Zahlbr.	Icmeri	13	9	1	0	0	2	U	C
Imshaugia aleurites (Ach.) S. F. Meyer	Imsale	2	0	0	2	3	0	U	M
Lasallia pensylvanica (Hoffm.) Llano	Laspen	3	0	1	3	0	0	U	M
Lecanora dispersa (Pers.) Sommerf.	Lecdis	1	0	0	0	0	1	U	C
Lecanora epibryon (Ach.) Ach.	Lecepi	5	0	0	0	0	5	U	C
Lecanora fuscescens (Sommerf.) Nyl.	Lecfus	1	0	0	0	0	1	U	C
Lecanora luteovernalis Brodo	Leclut	3	0	0	0	0	3	U	C
Lecanora symmicta s.l. (Ach.) Ach.	Lecsym	1	0	0	0	0	1	U	C
Lecidea sp. Ach.	Led	3	0	0	0	0	3	U	C
Lecidea albohyalina (Nyl.) Th. Fr.	Ledalb	1	0	0	0	0	1	U	C
Lecidea diapensiae Th. Fr.	Leddia	2	0	0	0	0	2	U	C
Lecidea lactea Flörke ex Schaerer	Ledlac	1	0	0	0	0	1	U	C
Lecidea plana (J. Lahm) Nyl.	Ledpla	1	0	0	0	0	1	U	C
Lecidea ramulosa Th. Fr.	Ledram	1	0	0	0	0	1	U	C
Leciophysma sp. Th. Fr.	Lei	1	0	0	0	3	0	U	C
Leciophysma finmarkicum Th. Fr.	Leifin	5	0	0	0	0	5	U	C
Lecidella euphorea (Flörke) Hertel	Leleup	1	0	0	0	0	1	U	C
Lecidella wulfenii (Hepp) Körber	Lelwul	1	0	0	0	0	1	U	C
Lempholemma sp. Körber	Lem	1	0	0	0	0	1	U	C
Lempholemma polyanthes (Bernh.) Malme	Lempol	1	0	0	0	3	0	U	C
Leproloma diffusum J. R. Laundon	Leodif	1	0	0	0	0	1	U	C
Leptogium sp. (Ach.) Gray	Lep	7	0	0	10	0	1	U	M

39

Appendix 1. Lichen species list from 445 plots within ARCN, including 351 macrolichens, 138 microlichens and 2 basidiolichens (continued).

Species	Code	Freq	Within Park Frequency (% plots)					Rarity	Form
			BELA	CAKR	GAAR	KOVA	NOAT		
Leptogium arcticum P. M. Jørg.	Leparc	1	0	0	0	0	1	U	M
Leptogium lichenoides (L.) Zahlbr.	Leplic	9	0	0	3	8	4	U	M
Leptogium saturninum (Dickson) Nyl.	Lepsat	23	0	1	11	13	8	O	M
Leptogium schraderi (Ach.) Nyl.	Lepsch	1	0	0	0	0	1	U	M
Leptogium tenuissimum (Dickson) Körber	Lepten	3	0	1	0	5	0	U	M
Leucocarpia biatorella (Arnold) Vězda (Buck & Harris 2001)	Leubia	1	0	0	0	0	1	U	C
Lobaria kurokawae Yoshim.	Lobkur	8	0	1	0	3	5	U	M
Lobaria linita (Ach.) Rabenh.	Loblin	99	20	14	17	42	30	C	M
Lobaria pseudopulmonaria Gyelnik	Lobpse	30	0	20	0	0	3	O	M
Lobaria pulmonaria (L.) Hoffm.	Lobpul	1	0	0	0	0	1	U	M
Lobaria scrobiculata (Scop.) DC.	Lobscr	20	0	6	3	8	6	O	M
Lopadium sp. Körber	Lop	2	0	0	0	0	2	U	C
Lopadium coralloideum (Nyl.) Lynge	Lopcor	3	0	1	0	3	1	U	C
Lopadium pezizoideum (Ach.) Körber	Loppez	3	0	0	0	0	3	U	C
Masonhalea richardsonii (Hook.) Kärnefelt	Mahric	67	8	7	14	29	26	C	M
Massalongia carnosa (Dickson) Körber	Mascar	4	0	0	0	5	2	U	M
Megaspora verrucosa (Ach.) Hafellner & V. Wirth	Megver	3	0	0	0	0	3	U	C
Melanohalea exasperatula (De Not.) O. Blanco	Mehexa	5	0	0	8	0	0	U	M
Melanohalea olivacea (L.) O. Blanco et al.	Meholi	5	0	1	3	3	0	U	M
Melanohalea olivaceoides (Krog) O. Blanco et al.	Meholo	3	0	0	5	0	0	U	M
Melanohalea septentrionalis (Lynge) O. Blanco	Mehsep	95	0	59	8	18	3	C	M
Melanelia sp. Essl.	Mel	2	0	1	0	0	0	U	M
Melanelia agnata (Nyl.) Thell	Melagn	7	0	2	0	8	1	U	M
Melanelia disjuncta (Erichsen) Essl.	Meldis	7	0	0	5	8	1	U	M
Melanelia panniformis (Nyl.) Essl.	Melpan	18	0	2	11	13	3	O	M
Melanelia sorediata (Ach.) Goward & Ahti	Melsor	7	0	1	2	8	2	U	M
Melanelia stygia (L.) Essl.	Melsty	29	3	2	14	21	5	O	M
Melanelia tominii (Oksner) Essl.	Meltom	7	0	0	10	0	1	U	M
Melanelia trabeculata (Ahti) Essl.	Meltra	7	0	0	0	11	3	U	M

Appendix 1. Lichen species list from 445 plots within ARCN, including 351 macrolichens, 138 microlichens and 2 basidiolichens (continued).

Species	Code	Freq	Within Park Frequency (% plots)					Rarity	Form
			BELA	CAKR	GAAR	KOVA	NOAT		
Micarea sp. Fr.	Mic	2	0	0	0	0	2	U	C
Micarea crassipes (Th. Fr.) Coppins	Miccra	1	0	0	0	0	1	U	C
Micarea incrassata Hedl.	Micinc	1	0	0	0	0	1	U	C
Micarea ternaria (Nyl.) Vězda	Micter	2	0	0	0	0	2	U	C
Multiclavula vernalis (Schwein.) R. Petersen	Mulver	3	0	0	0	0	3	U	B
Mycoblastus alpinus (Fr.) Kernst.	Mycalp	1	0	0	0	0	1	U	C
Mycobilimbia sp. Rehm	Mym	1	0	0	0	0	1	U	C
Mycobilimbia berengeriana (A. Massal.) Hafellner & V. Wirth	Mymber	1	0	0	0	0	1	U	C
Mycobilimbia carneoalbida (Müll. Arg.) S. Ekman (Ekman 2004c)	Mymcar	1	0	0	0	0	1	U	C
Mycobilimbia hypnorum (Lib.) Kalb & Hafellner	Mymhyp	6	0	0	0	0	5	U	C
Mycobilimbia obscurata (Sommerf.) Rehm	Mymobs	1	0	0	0	0	1	U	C
Nephroma sp. Ach.	Nep	1	0	1	0	0	0	U	M
Nephroma arcticum (L.) Torss.	Neparc	105	22	25	14	34	24	C	M
Nephroma bellum (Sprengel) Tuck.	Nepbel	24	0	4	8	5	10	O	M
Nephroma expallidum (Nyl.) Nyl.	Nepexp	96	12	28	17	21	24	C	M
Nephroma helveticum Ach.	Nephel	8	0	0	5	8	2	U	M
Nephroma isidiosum (Nyl.) Gyelnik	Nepisi	2	0	1	0	0	0	U	M
Nephroma parile (Ach.) Ach.	Neppar	20	1	4	6	8	6	O	M
Nephroma resupinatum (L.) Ach.	Nepres	4	0	0	6	0	0	U	M
Ochrolechia sp. A. Massal.	Och	5	0	0	0	0	5	U	C
Ochrolechia androgyna (Hoffm.) Arnold	Ochand	1	0	0	0	0	1	U	C
Ochrolechia frigida (Sw.) Lynge(Räsänen) Hafellner & R. W. Rogers	Ochfri	27	2	9	0	0	12	O	C
Ochrolechia gyalectina (Nyl.) Zahlbr.	Ochgya	1	0	0	0	0	1	U	C
Ochrolechia inaequatula (Nyl.) Zahlbr.	Ochina	1	0	0	0	0	1	U	C
Ochrolechia upsaliensis (L.) A. Massal.	Ochups	2	0	0	0	0	2	U	C
Omphalina umbellifera (L. : Fr.) Quélet	Ompumb	1	0	0	0	0	1	U	B

Appendix 1. Lichen species list from 445 plots within ARCN, including 351 macrolichens, 138 microlichens and 2 basidiolichens (continued).

Species	Code	Freq	Within Park Frequency (% plots)					Rarity	Form
			BELA	CAKR	GAAR	KOVA	NOAT		
Ophioparma sp. Norman	Oph	1	0	0	0	0	1	U	C
Ophioparma ventosa (L.) Norman (May 1997)	Ophven	1	0	0	0	0	1	U	C
Orphniospora moriopsis (A. Massal.) D. Hawksw.	Orpmor	2	0	0	0	0	2	U	C
Pannaria sp. Delise	Pan	2	0	1	0	0	0	U	M
Pannaria conoplea (Ach.) Bory	Pancon	4	0	1	0	0	3	U	M
Parmeliopsis ambigua (Wulfen) Nyl.	Papamb	74	7	30	5	32	10	C	M
Parmeliopsis hyperopta (Ach.) Arnold	Paphyp	101	1	46	8	37	17	C	M
Parmelia sp. Ach.	Par	1	0	1	0	0	0	U	M
Parmelia fraudans (Nyl.) Nyl.	Parfra	3	0	0	3	3	0	U	M
Parmelia hygrophila Goward & Ahti	Parhyg	1	0	0	0	3	0	U	M
Parmelia omphalodes (L.) Ach.	Paromp	82	9	21	22	26	18	C	M
Parmelia saxatilis (L.) Ach. (L.) Ach.	Parsax	14	0	4	5	11	2	O	M
Parmelia squarrosa Hale	Parsqu	6	0	1	0	8	1	U	M
Parmelia sulcata Taylor	Parsul	96	13	35	16	32	13	C	M
Peltigera sp. Willd.	Pel	14	0	5	2	11	2	O	M
Peltigera aphthosa (L.) Willd.	Pelaph	161	21	59	19	8	41	C	M
Peltigera britannica (Gyelnik) Holt-Hartw. & Tønsberg	Pelbri	2	0	0	0	5	0	U	M
Peltigera canina (L.) Willd.	Pelcan	36	1	7	17	5	12	O	M
Peltigera cinnamomea Goward	Pelcin	1	0	1	0	0	0	U	M
Peltigera collina (Ach.) Schrader	Pelcol	2	0	1	0	0	1	U	M
Peltigera didactyla (With.) J. R. Laundon	Peldid	34	0	13	5	13	7	O	M
Peltigera elisabethae Gyelnik	Peleli	4	0	1	0	8	0	U	M
Peltigera extenuata (Vain.) Lojka (Goffinet et al 2003)	Pelext	10	0	0	0	0	9	U	M
Peltigera horizontalis (Hudson) Baumg.	Pelhor	4	1	0	0	0	3	U	M
Peltigera kristinssonii Vitik.	Pelkri	17	0	7	2	3	5	O	M
Peltigera lepidophora (Vainio) Bitter	Pellep	5	0	0	0	5	3	U	M
Peltigera leucophlebia (Nyl.) Gyelnik	Pelleu	102	19	26	2	39	29	C	M

Appendix 1. Lichen species list from 445 plots within ARCN, including 351 macrolichens, 138 microlichens and 2 basidiolichens (continued).

Species	Code	Freq	Within Park Frequency (% plots)					Rarity	Form
			BELA	CAKR	GAAR	KOVA	NOAT		
Peltigera malacea (Ach.) Funck	Pelmal	53	2	17	16	16	11	C	M
Peltigera membranacea (Ach.) Nyl.	Pelmem	14	1	4	2	0	5	O	M
Peltigera neckeri Hepp ex Müll. Arg.	Pelnec	5	1	1	0	5	1	U	M
Peltigera neopolydactyla (Gyelnik) Gyelnik	Pelneo	10	2	0	0	0	7	U	M
Peltigera occidentalis (Dahl) Krist.	Pelocc	3	0	0	0	3	2	U	M
Peltigera polydactylon (Necker) Hoffm.	Pelpol	75	3	38	3	3	16	C	M
Peltigera ponojensis Gyelnik	Pelpon	6	0	1	0	0	5	U	M
Peltigera praetextata (Flörke ex Sommerf.) Zopf	Pelpra	4	1	0	2	0	2	U	M
Peltigera rufescens (Weiss) Humb.	Pelruf	66	3	9	13	37	26	C	M
Peltigera scabrosa Th. Fr.	Pelsca	129	17	49	11	18	29	C	M
Peltigera venosa (L.) Hoffm. (L.) Hoffm.	Pelven	5	0	1	0	3	3	U	M
Pertusaria sp. DC.	Per	3	0	0	0	0	3	U	C
Pertusaria alaskensis Erichsen	Perala	1	0	0	0	0	1	U	C
Pertusaria bryontha (Ach.) Nyl.	Perbry	2	0	0	0	0	2	U	C
Pertusaria dactylina (Ach.) Nyl.	Perdac	13	0	4	2	0	5	U	C
Pertusaria geminipara (Th. Fr.) C. Knight ex Brodo	Pergem	2	0	0	0	0	2	U	C
Pertusaria oculata (Dickson) Th. Fr.	Perocu	1	0	0	0	0	1	U	C
Pertusaria panyrga (Ach.) A. Massal.	Perpan	3	0	0	0	0	3	U	C
Pertusaria sommerfeltii (Flörke ex Sommerf.) Fr.	Persom	1	0	0	0	0	1	U	C
Pertusaria subdactylina Nyl.	Persub	2	0	0	0	0	2	U	C
Phaeophyscia sp. Moberg	Pha	1	0	0	0	0	1	U	M
Phaeophyscia ciliata (Hoffm.) Moberg	Phacil	1	0	0	2	0	0	U	M
Phaeophyscia constipata (Norrlin & Nyl.) Moberg	Phacon	2	0	0	2	0	1	U	M
Phaeophyscia decolor (Kashiw.) Essl.	Phadec	3	0	1	3	0	0	U	M
Phaeophyscia endococcina (Körber) Moberg	Phaend	2	0	0	3	0	0	U	M
Phaeophyscia hirsuta (Mereschk.) Essl.	Phahir	1	0	0	0	3	0	U	M
Phaeophyscia kairamoi (Vainio) Moberg	Phakai	6	0	0	3	8	1	U	M
Phaeophyscia orbicularis (Necker) Moberg	Phaorb	1	0	0	0	3	0	U	M
Phaeophyscia sciastra (Ach.) Moberg	Phasci	5	0	1	3	3	1	U	M

Appendix 1. Lichen species list from 445 plots within ARCN, including 351 macrolichens, 138 microlichens and 2 basidiolichens (continued).

Species	Code	Freq	Within Park Frequency (% plots)					Rarity	Form
			BELA	CAKR	GAAR	KOVA	NOAT		
Physconia sp. Poelt	Phc	1	0	1	0	0	0	U	M
Physconia detersa (Nyl.) Poelt	Phcdet	1	0	0	0	3	0	U	M
Physconia muscigena (Ach.) Poelt	Phcmus	28	0	3	19	11	7	O	M
Physconia perisidiosa (Erichsen) Moberg	Phcper	4	0	1	0	8	0	U	M
Physcia sp. (Schreber) Michaux	Phy	3	0	1	0	3	1	U	M
Physcia adscendens (Fr.) H. Olivier	Phyads	2	0	0	2	3	0	U	M
Physcia aipolia (Ehrh. ex Humb.) Fürnr.	Phyaip	17	0	4	13	0	3	O	M
Physcia caesia (Hoffm.) Fürnr.	Phycae	20	0	1	13	11	5	O	M
Physcia dubia (Hoffm.) Lettau	Phydub	7	0	0	8	3	1	U	M
Physcia phaea (Tuck.) J. W. Thomson	Phypha	6	0	0	8	0	1	U	M
Phaeorrhiza sp. H. Mayrh. & Poelt	Phz	1	0	0	0	0	1	U	C
Pilophorus cereolus (Ach.) Th. Fr. in Hellb.	Pilcer	7	3	0	0	3	3	U	M
Pilophorus robustus Th. Fr.	Pilrob	8	1	0	2	8	3	U	M
Pilophorus vegae Krog	Pilveg	1	0	0	0	0	1	U	M
Placynthium asperellum (Ach.) Trevisan	Plaasp	1	0	0	0	0	1	U	M
Placynthium nigrum (Hudson) Gray	Planig	8	0	1	0	5	4	U	M
Placidium sp. A. Massal. (Breuss 1996)	Pld	1	0	0	0	0	1	U	M
Placidium norvegicum (Breuss) Breuss	Pldnor	1	0	0	0	0	1	U	M
Pleopsidium sp. Körber	Ple	1	0	0	0	0	1	U	C
Placopsis cribellans (Nyl.) Räsänen	Plpcri	1	0	0	0	0	1	U	C
Placopsis gelida (L.) Lindsay	Plpgel	1	0	0	0	0	1	U	C
Placopsis lambii Hertel & V. Wirth (1987)	Plplam	1	0	0	0	0	1	U	C
Placynthiella sp. Elenkin	Ply	1	0	0	0	0	1	U	C
Placynthiella icmalea (Ach.) Coppins & P. James	Plyicm	5	0	0	0	0	5	U	C
Placynthiella oligotropha (J. R. Laundon) Coppins & P. James	Plyoli	1	0	0	0	0	1	U	C
Placynthiella uliginosa (Schrader) Coppins & P. James	Plyuli	4	0	0	0	3	3	U	C
Polyblastia terrestris Th. Fr.	Pobter	2	0	0	0	0	2	U	C
Polychidium muscicola (Sw.) Gray	Polmus	1	0	0	0	0	1	U	M

Appendix 1. Lichen species list from 445 plots within ARCN, including 351 macrolichens, 138 microlichens and 2 basidiolichens (continued).

Species	Code	Freq	Within Park Frequency (% plots)					Rarity	Form
			BELA	CAKR	GAAR	KOVA	NOAT		
Porpidia sp. Körber	Por	1	0	0	0	0	1	U	C
Porpidia crustulata (Ach.) Hertel & Knoph	Porcru	1	0	0	0	0	1	U	C
Porpidia flavocaerulescens (Hornem.) Hertel & A. J. Schwab	Porfla	2	0	0	0	0	2	U	C
Porpidia grisea Gowan	Porgri	1	0	0	0	0	1	U	C
Porpidia speirea (Ach.) Kremp.	Porspe	1	0	0	0	0	1	U	C
Porpidia superba (Körber) Hertel & Knoph	Porsup	1	0	0	0	0	1	U	C
Porpidia thomsonii Gowan	Portho	2	0	0	0	0	2	U	C
Porpidia tuberculosa (Sm.) Hertel & Knoph	Portub	1	0	0	0	0	1	U	C
Protoparmelia badia (Hoffm.) Hafellner	Prabad	1	0	0	0	0	1	U	C
Protoblastenia rupestris (Scop.) J. Steiner	Prbrup	1	0	0	0	0	1	U	C
Protopannaria pezizoides (Weber) P. M. Jørg. (Jørgensen 2000)	Propez	16	0	7	8	3	0	O	M
Pseudocyphellaria crocata (L.) Vainio	Psccro	1	0	0	0	0	1	U	M
Pseudephebe minuscula (Nyl. ex Arnold) Brodo & D. Hawksw.	Psemin	22	3	1	10	29	0	O	M
Pseudephebe pubescens (L.) M. Choisy	Psepub	26	2	2	14	3	10	O	M
Psoroma hypnorum (Vahl) Gray	Psmhyp	53	0	25	6	26	5	C	M
Psora sp. Hoffm.	Pso	5	0	0	6	0	1	U	M
Psora cerebriformis W. A. Weber	Psocer	1	0	0	0	0	1	U	M
Psora decipiens (Hedwig) Hoffm.	Psodec	6	1	1	0	5	2	U	M
Psora himalayana (Church. Bab.) Timdal	Psohim	2	0	0	0	0	2	U	M
Psora nipponica (Zahlbr.) Gotth. Schneider	Psonip	1	1	0	0	0	0	U	M
Psora rubiformis (Ach.) Hook.	Psorub	1	0	0	0	0	1	U	M
Psora tuckermanii R. Anderson ex Timdal	Psotuc	2	0	0	3	0	0	U	M
Pyrenopsis grumulifera Nyl.	Pyrgru	1	0	0	0	0	1	U	C
Ramalina sp. Ach.	Ram	2	0	0	0	5	0	U	M
Ramalina almquistii Vainio	Ramalm	13	4	4	0	3	3	U	M
Ramalina dilacerata (Hoffm.) Hoffm.	Ramdil	9	0	1	6	8	0	U	M

Appendix 1. Lichen species list from 445 plots within ARCN, including 351 macrolichens, 138 microlichens and 2 basidiolichens (continued).

Species	Code	Freq	Within Park Frequency (% plots)					Rarity	Form
			BELA	CAKR	GAAR	KOVA	NOAT		
Ramalina intermedia (Delise ex Nyl.) Nyl.	Ramint	1	1	0	0	0	0	U	M
Ramalina pollinaria (Westr.) Ach.	Rampol	1	0	0	0	0	1	U	M
Ramalina roesleri (Hochst. ex Schaerer) Hue	Ramroe	17	0	3	3	13	5	O	M
Ramalina sinensis Jatta	Ramsin	3	0	0	0	0	3	U	M
Ramalina thrausta (Ach.) Nyl.	Ramthr	2	0	0	0	0	2	U	M
Rhizoplaca chrysoleuca (Sm.) Zopf	Rhichr	5	0	0	8	0	0	U	C
Rhizoplaca melanophthalma (DC.) Leuckert & Poelt	Rhimel	2	0	0	3	0	0	U	C
Rhizocarpon sp. Ramond ex DC.	Rhp	3	0	0	0	0	3	U	C
Rhizocarpon chioneum (Norman) Th. Fr.	Rhpchi	1	0	0	0	0	1	U	C
Rhizocarpon cinereovirens (Müll. Arg.) Vainio	Rhpcin	1	0	0	0	0	1	U	C
Rhizocarpon cumulatum J. W. Thomson	Rhpcum	1	0	0	0	0	1	U	C
Rhizocarpon eupetraeoides (Nyl.) Blomb. & Forss.	Rhpeuo	1	0	0	0	0	1	U	C
Rhizocarpon eupetraeum (Nyl.) Arnold	Rhpeup	1	0	0	0	0	1	U	C
Rhizocarpon expallescens Th. Fr.	Rhpexp	1	0	0	0	0	1	U	C
Rhizocarpon geographicum (L.) DC.	Rhpgeo	2	0	0	2	0	1	U	C
Rhizocarpon rubescens Th. Fr. (fide Fryday)	Rhprub	1	0	0	0	0	1	U	C
Rimularia limborina Nyl.	Rimlim	1	0	0	0	0	1	U	C
Rinodina sp. (Ach.) Gray	Rin	3	0	0	0	0	3	U	C
Rinodina bischoffii (Hepp) A. Massal.	Rinbis	1	0	0	0	0	1	U	C
Rinodina mniaraea (Ach.) Körber	Rinmni	3	0	0	0	0	3	U	C
Rinodina olivaceobrunnea C. W. Dodge & Baker	Rinoli	1	0	0	0	0	1	U	C
Rinodina roscida (Sommerf.) Arnold	Rinros	2	0	0	0	0	2	U	C
Rinodina septentrionalis Malme	Rinsep	1	0	0	0	0	1	U	C
Rinodina turfacea (Wahlenb.) Körber	Rintur	2	0	0	0	0	2	U	C
Ropalospora lugubris (Sommerf.) Poelt	Roplug	1	0	0	0	0	1	U	C
Sarcogyne sp. Flotow	Sar	1	0	0	0	0	1	U	C
Sarcosagium campestre (Fr.) Poetsch & Schiedem.	Sascam	1	0	0	0	0	1	U	C

Species	Code	Freq	Within Park Frequency (% plots)					Rarity	Form
			BELA	CAKR	GAAR	KOVA	NOAT		
Siphula ceratites (Wahlenb.) Fr.	Sipcer	7	6	0	0	0	1	U	M
Solorina sp. Ach.	Sol	1	0	0	0	0	1	U	M
Solorina bispora Nyl.	Solbis	39	2	1	3	5	28	O	M
Solorina crocea (L.) Ach.	Solcro	23	3	0	10	13	8	O	M
Solorina octospora (Arnold) Arnold	Soloct	1	0	0	0	3	0	U	M
Solorina saccata (L.) Ach.	Solsac	10	0	1	3	16	1	U	M
Solorina spongiosa (Ach.) Anzi	Solspo	4	0	0	0	5	2	U	M
Sphaerophorus fragilis (L.) Pers.	Sphfra	51	21	6	11	18	7	C	M
Sphaerophorus globosus (Hudson) Vainio	Sphglo	154	68	29	19	26	23	C	M
Squamarina lentigera (Weber) Poelt	Squlen	2	0	0	0	5	0	U	M
Stereocaulon sp. Hoffm.	Ste	6	0	1	2	0	3	U	M
Stereocaulon alpestre (Flot.) Dombr.	Steale	2	0	0	0	3	1	U	M
Stereocaulon alpinum Laurer ex Funck	Stealp	43	2	4	17	21	14	O	M
Stereocaulon apocalypticum Nyl.	Steapc	14	3	0	2	11	5	O	M
Stereocaulon arcticum Lynge	Stearc	1	0	0	0	0	1	U	M
Stereocaulon arenarium (Savicz) Lamb	Steare	2	1	0	0	0	1	U	M
Stereocaulon botryosum Ach.	Stebot	14	1	0	6	11	5	O	M
Stereocaulon condensatum Hoffm.	Stecod	1	0	0	0	3	0	U	M
Stereocaulon glareosum (Savicz) H. Magn.	Stegla	8	1	1	6	0	2	U	M
Stereocaulon grande (H. Magn.) H. Magn.	Stegra	1	0	1	0	0	0	U	M
Stereocaulon groenlandicum (E. Dahl) Lamb	Stegro	9	2	1	0	8	3	U	M
Stereocaulon intermedium (Savicz) H. Magn.	Steint	3	0	0	3	0	1	U	M
Stereocaulon paschale (L.) Hoffm.	Stepas	91	33	17	6	26	20	C	M
Stereocaulon rivulorum H. Magn.	Steriv	7	0	4	2	0	1	U	M
Stereocaulon saviczii Du Rietz	Stesav	1	0	0	2	0	0	U	M
Stereocaulon saxatile H. Magn.	Stesax	1	0	0	2	0	0	U	M
Stereocaulon species 1	Stesp1	2	0	0	0	3	1	U	M
Stereocaulon species 2	Stesp2	2	0	0	0	5	0	U	M

Appendix 1. Lichen species list from 445 plots within ARCN, including 351 macrolichens, 138 microlichens and 2 basidiolichens (continued).

Species	Code	Freq	Within Park Frequency (% plots)					Rarity	Form
			BELA	CAKR	GAAR	KOVA	NOAT		
Stereocaulon spathuliferum Vainio	Stespa	1	0	0	0	0	1	U	M
Stereocaulon subcoralloides (Nyl.) Nyl.	Stesub	30	4	2	5	24	10	O	M
Stereocaulon symphycheilum Lamb	Stesym	17	7	0	0	13	5	O	M
Stereocaulon tomentosum Fr.	Stetom	26	4	4	17	0	5	O	M
Stereocaulon vesuvianum Pers.	Steves	4	2	0	0	0	2	U	M
Stereocaulon wrightii Tuck.	Stewri	2	2	0	0	0	0	U	M
Sticta arctica Degel.	Stiarc	7	3	0	0	0	4	U	M
Thamnolia sp. Ach. ex Schaerer	Tha	1	0	0	0	0	1	U	M
Thamnolia subuliformis (Ehrh.) Culb.	Thasub	205	33	72	14	58	40	C	M
Thamnolia vermicularis (Sw.) Ach. ex Schaerer	Thaver	122	60	12	2	29	32	C	M
Thrombium epigaeum (Pers.) Wallr.	Threpi	1	0	0	0	0	1	U	C
Toninia aromatica (Sm.) A. Massal.	Tonaro	1	0	0	0	0	1	U	C
Trapeliopsis granulosa (Hoffm.) Lumbsch	Tragra	2	0	0	0	0	2	U	C
Tremolecia atrata (Ach.) Hertel	Treatr	1	0	0	0	0	1	U	C
Tuckermannopsis chlorophylla (Willd.) Hale	Tucchl	1	0	0	2	0	0	U	M
Umbilicaria sp. Hoffm.	Umb	1	0	0	0	0	1	U	M
Umbilicaria angulata Tuck.	Umbang	2	0	0	0	5	0	U	M
Umbilicaria arctica (Ach.) Nyl.	Umbarc	7	5	0	2	0	1	U	M
Umbilicaria caroliniana Tuck.	Umbcar	34	12	1	16	21	2	O	M
Umbilicaria cinereorufescens (Schaerer) Frey	Umbcin	7	0	0	11	0	0	U	M
Umbilicaria cylindrica (L.) Delise ex Duby	Umbcyl	14	1	0	13	8	2	O	M
Umbilicaria deusta (L.) Baumg.	Umbdeu	8	0	0	6	8	1	U	M
Umbilicaria hyperborea var. hyperborea (Ach.) Hoffm.	Umbhyp	39	10	4	16	32	2	O	M
Umbilicaria hyperborea var. radicicula (J. E. Zetterst.) Hasselrot	Umbhyr	7	0	1	0	0	5	U	M
Umbilicaria phaea Tuck.	Umbpha	1	0	0	0	0	1	U	M
Umbilicaria polyphylla (L.) Baumg.	Umbpol	2	1	0	0	0	1	U	M
Umbilicaria proboscidea (L.) Schrader	Umbpro	56	20	3	24	24	7	C	M

Appendix 1. Lichen species list from 445 plots within ARCN, including 351 macrolichens, 138 microlichens and 2 basidiolichens (continued).

Species	Code	Freq	Within Park Frequency (% plots)					Rarity	Form
			BELA	CAKR	GAAR	KOVA	NOAT		
Umbilicaria rigida (Du Rietz) Frey	Umbrig	2	2	0	0	0	0	U	M
Umbilicaria scholanderi (Llano) Krog	Umbsch	1	1	0	0	0	0	U	M
Umbilicaria torrefacta (Lightf.) Schrader	Umbtor	22	3	3	3	16	6	O	M
Umbilicaria vellea (L.) Hoffm.	Umbvel	3	0	0	2	5	0	U	M
Umbilicaria virginis Schaerer	Umbvir	1	0	0	0	3	0	U	M
Usnea sp. Dill. ex Adans.	Usn	2	0	0	0	5	0	U	M
Usnea lapponica Vainio	Usnlap	4	0	0	5	3	0	U	M
Usnea longissima Ach.	Usnlon	1	0	0	0	3	0	U	M
Usnea scabrata Nyl.	Usnsca	3	0	0	5	0	0	U	M
Usnea subfloridana Stirton	Usnsub	1	0	0	2	0	0	U	M
Varicellaria rhodocarpa (Körber) Th. Fr.	Varrho	3	0	0	0	0	3	U	C
Verrucaria sp. Schrader	Ver	2	0	0	0	0	2	U	C
Vestergrenopsis elaeina (Wahlenb.) Gyelnik	Vesela	1	0	0	0	0	1	U	M
Vestergrenopsis isidiata (Degel.) E. Dahl	Vesisi	1	0	0	2	0	0	U	M
Xanthoria candelaria (L.) Th. Fr.	Xancan	4	0	0	3	5	0	U	M
Xanthoria elegans (Link) Th. Fr.	Xanele	11	0	1	13	3	1	U	M
Xanthoria polycarpa (Hoffm.) Rieber	Xanpol	1	0	0	0	0	1	U	M
Xanthoria sorediata (Vainio) Poelt	Xansor	2	0	0	2	0	1	U	M
Xanthoparmelia coloradoensis (Gyelnik) Hale	Xapcol	4	0	0	5	0	1	U	M
Xanthomendoza borealis (R. Sant. & Poelt) Søchting, Kärnefelt & S. Kondr.	Xazbor	2	0	0	0	0	2	U	M
Xanthomendoza oregana (Gyelnik) Søchting, Kärnefelt & S. Kondr.	Xazore	1	0	1	0	0	0	U	M

Freq represents the number of plots in which the species occurs (out of 445 total).
Rarity levels are: Uncommon (ARCN-wide frequency of 0-2%), Occasional (3-9%), Common (10-50%) or Abundant (>51%).
Form indicates the lichen growth form: M – Macrolichen, C – Crustose lichen (microlichen), or B – Basidiolichen.
[1]T. Ahti synonmized *Cladonia scotteri*, *C. symphycarpia* and *C. symphycarpa* into one taxon in McCune et al. 2009, but we have retained as three separate species here until further taxonomic study.

49

NPS 953/105821, November 2010